Summit's Courthouse

Summit's Courthouse

Its Past, Pictures and People

By Susan Donaldson

P.O. Box 745
Breckenridge, CO 80424-0745
(970) 453-9022; fax (970) 453-8135

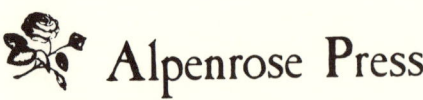

P.O. Box 499
Silverthorne, CO 80498-0499
(970) 468-6273

Summit County Courthouse
Breckenridge, Colorado

So handsome is the Summit County Courthouse that many artists put its likeness on their work. The watercolor above graces the front of a notecard. The building also is featured on a teapot, on the Summit Historical Society's Year 2000 Christmas ornament, on a white, porcelain, gold-rimmed plate and on a 17" x 17" blue scarf. The plate and scarf are displayed at the historical society's 1896 William Harrison Briggle House at 104 North Harris Street in Breckenridge. Print courtesy of Larry Gilliland.

CONTENTS

SECTION II: THE PEOPLE

Author's Note

My husband has sub-subtitled this book *The Little Brochure That Grew*. The name is apt, for this book began as a pamphlet.

Early in 1999, the Summit County Public Arts Exhibit Committee (SCPAEC) produced a brochure on the artwork in the County Commons. It was such a hit with tourists and residents that county staff asked the committee to write a leaflet on the Summit County Courthouse. According to staff, the historic courthouse is visited frequently and, more often than not, visitors pepper employees with lots of questions. A brochure with information on the most commonly asked questions would be very helpful, staff said.

As a committee member, I volunteered to write the pamphlet -- an impossibility, I soon discovered. The impossible nature of the assignment lay in the vast quantity of information available -- too much to fit into a brochure yet too important to leave out. I mentioned this difficulty at a meeting, casually ending my report with the comment, "There's enough material to write a book."

"Then why not write a book?" asked County Commissioner Gary Lindstrom, also a SCPAEC member. My heart raced. Could I have heard correctly? I'd wanted to write a book for years. Could this truly be an opportunity to achieve that goal and do historical research -- pure pleasure for me -- simultaneously? The committee gave me its blessing to proceed. I eagerly immersed myself in the project. *Summit's Courthouse* is the result.

In addition to extending my sincere gratitude to the committee for its support and confidence in me, I'd like to recognize several individuals for their special assistance and encouragement. Mary Ellen Gilliland, my editor, has an enviable way with words. She very nicely forced me to rewrite and then rewrite again until my sentences were shorter and had more spark. County Commissioners Gary Lindstrom, Tom Long and Bill Wallace evidenced their faith in me by agreeing to cover the book's production cost. Gary Lindstrom and County Manager Bob Taylor spent valuable time taking me around the courthouse, explaining the musical-chairs history of the rooms. Maureen Nicholls spent hours poring over old Breckenridge maps with me. We even tape-measured parcels on Main Street! Maureen is a stickler for accuracy, and I benefited from her knowledge and penchant for detail. Despite the numerous phone calls I made to Bud Enyeart, ex-county commissioner, he was always courteous, patient and quick to share his remembrances. Paul Johnson researched the Search and Rescue effort and willingly shared his information with me. Summit County Sheriff Joe Morales took hours out of a busy day to answer questions and to enlighten me on jail procedures and incidents. My husband, Dave, rescued me several times when my computer froze after suddenly determining that I had -- horrors! -- committed some illegal procedure. Dave and Karen Musolf critiqued the final draft and made valuable suggestions.

I interviewed more than 70 individuals, too many to list, but I'm indebted to all for their comments so freely given. On the whole, people -- most of them strangers to me -- were enthusiastic and helpful. They made this experience a positive one. I hope readers enjoy reading the book as much as I enjoyed writing it.

S.D.

A humble wagoneer provides quite a contrast to the stately court-house beyond. A place of contrast, Summit County was home to this architectural triumph as well as home to the ordinary, hard-working taxpayer -- who footed part of the building's $43,000 price tag. On one matter, however, the diversity simply dissolved -- all were (and are) proud of the handsome structure that housed the county seat's offices.

Section I: The Building

Chapter One
The Courthouse

All the makings of a gripping mystery are here. A raid. The cover of darkness. A remote location. A hidden place for the loot. A suspect. Even a second heist attempt.

Mystery #1: The County Seat
Musical chairs.

Mystery clouds the early history of Summit County's seat of government. Frank Hall, author of the four-volume 1895 *History of the State of Colorado*, wrote: "From the beginning of local government its [Summit County's] county seat has been located at the town of Breckenridge."

Who would argue the county seat's Breckenridge location with this eminent historian? Plenty of other historians dispute the point, and even they disagree about the details. Yet others, such as Stanley Dempsey and James E. Fell in *Mining the Summit*, agree with Hall that Breckenridge has always served as the Summit County seat of government.

Recorded facts, however, must bear the most weight, and they contradict Hall, Dempsey and Fell. These facts state that on Nov. 1, 1861, the territory's First Legislative Assembly and its first governor, William Gilpin, declared Parkville, not Breckenridge, the Summit County seat. In fact, Parkville almost became Colorado's capital. On Feb. 28, 1861, when Colorado

Territory was established, Parkville lost to Golden its bid to become the territorial capital by only 11 votes.

No single building in Parkville housed the county proceedings. Instead, meetings took place in scattered locations. Commissioners held meetings and court hearings in Parkville's newly established Masonic Temple, Lodge No. 2. Minutes of the April 12, 1862 commissioner meeting record the appropriation of $7.50 to "Summit Lodge No. 2 of A.F. & A.M. for use of Hall and fuel" during the January and April terms. Other county offices shared space in the Park Hotel. Here lies another discrepancy -- one historian places the Park Hotel in Breckenridge, not Parkville.

Lodged in the lodge

Masonic Lodge No. 2 was the second of three lodges in the state (the first was in rival Golden) and the first lodge on the Western Slope. Built in 1861 by the Masons and dedicated on May 6 of that year by Parson John M. Chivington, the lodge occupied the building's top floor; the ground floor housed O.A. Whittemore's General Store.

Some historians claim that one or more Breckenridge residents, believing that their town's booming prosperity merited political supremacy, stole the county records from Parkville in a midnight raid in 1862. These citizens hid the purloined papers in a log cabin on land later occupied by the Enterline King Store.* Later they moved the papers to the Silverthorn Hotel, on the west side of Main Street, for a short stay. Parkville authorities, told they could keep the county records if they could find them, searched unsuccessfully for the papers.

* The July 31, 1909 Summit County Journal places the Enterline King Store on the west side of North Main Street, while the Sept. 26, 1886 Daily Journal puts it on Lincoln Avenue.

While the papers were stashed in her hotel, Agnes Silverthorn thwarted a second theft of the records, this time by the county clerk who planned to return them to Parkville. Wallace La Baw, author of *Nah-oon-kara,* suggests that the "loved and kindly" Mrs. Silverthorn, the "good Samaritan to all in trouble and distress," might have instigated the theft of the records from Parkville in the first place!

Other historians state that the Board of County Commissioners (BOCC), on Jan. 6, 1862, decided to move the county seat to Breckenridge from Parkville. (The minutes of that meeting neither credit nor discredit that contention, for nothing about a move is recorded.) These historians make no mention of the moonlight heist.*

According to some chroniclers, the last county meeting in Parkville was held in March 1862. Others contend that meetings fluctuated between Breckenridge and Parkville from April 1862 to June 1864. The April 22, May 20 and Aug. 11, 1862 BOCC minutes record the appropriation of mileage reimbursement to commissioner Peter Mulhebach for his travels between the two towns. County meeting minutes list Breckenridge as the meeting site as of Feb. 9, 1863. The commissioners, at that meeting, ordered that a building suitable for a courthouse be erected immediately, under BOCC supervision.

The Feb. 9, 1863 order to build a courthouse was not the first such order. Less than a year earlier, on April 12, 1862, the commissioners ordered Joseph Thatcher, clerk of the board, "to issue notices for proposals to erect a suitable building for offices and courtroom."

* One historian totally dismisses the idea of a midnight raid, calling it preposterous. Most likely, she says, the heist took place during the day when court was in session in Breckenridge and no one was "minding the store" in Parkville.

Construction bids were due only nine days later, on April 21. Presumably, no bids were received. After all their effort in detailing the design, the commissioners found themselves at a meeting the next day discussing renewal of the A.F. and A.M. Society's hall as a courthouse.*

Working with Society officers M.C. White, A.B. Brown, Joseph Thatcher and O.A. Whittemore, the commissioners agreed to a rental-fee schedule. Charges included: $1/day for probate court, $1/day for county commissioner court and $3/day for district court. Fees were to be paid monthly on a use basis. In addition, $1/day would be charged for Hall use for all other county purposes.

Space needs for county government must have grown beyond what the Masonic Hall could accommodate, thus reinforcing the Hall's use as temporary, for at that April 22 meeting the commissioners authorized Thatcher to fix up a building situated between a hotel** and Charles H. Williams's house. The house was "denominated the Picture Gallery for the purposes of county clerk." The BOCC also empowered the county attorney to fix up a suitable room for his purposes. Possibly the structure sandwiched between Williams's house and the hotel

---

* Perhaps no bids were received because of the numerous specifications for the frame or log courthouse, which had to be 30′ x 40′ and have two stories. The lower story was to be 8 1/2′ "in the clear," the upper floor 10′ "in the clear." The rafters were not to be less than 6″ deep and 2′ apart. Roof shingles had to be 16″ long and "lain not over 5″ to the weather." The floor was to be of 1 1/4″ boards, not over 8″ wide, thoroughly seasoned and jointed.

There was to be one flight of stairs, with steps not over 8″ high nor less than 12″ wide. The steps had to be of 2″ plank. The width of the stairs was to be 5′. In the lower story the building had to have six windows and two outside doors, one front and one back. The upper-story windows had to be the same size as the ones below. There had to be three inside doors to the upper floor as well as two inside office doors on the lower level.

** The hand-written meeting records are illegible; the hotel's name could be Loncray, Conway, Toncray or ?

was the Park Hotel, for, according to BOCC minutes, on May 20, 1862, the commissioners appropriated $125 for the hotel's purchase.

No doubt about it, Parkville served as the county seat for a short while. The *Summit County Journal,* in a Jan. 4, 1908 article, referred to Samuel Woodhurst as the first county judge at Parkville. More authoritatively, minutes of the Jan. 6, April 22 and July 7, 1862 county commissioner meetings state that officials "met at Parkville, the county seat." There's no reason to believe that the meetings between those dates as well as all other meetings until Feb. 9, 1863, were held anywhere but in Parkville. References to Parkville as the first county seat are numerous.

Mystery #2: First County Office in Breckenridge
Here it is! No, there it is!

Another debate arises over what building in Breckenridge housed the county's first office. Three structures vie for that honor. Following are the contestants.

✦ **Pollock's Cabin**
The first county building was William P. Pollock's 1862 log cabin on North Main Street. According to Lois Theobald in *Thar's GOLD in them thar hills!,* that is where the filched papers were hidden. Appropriately, Pollock was the county's first clerk and recorder. (Or was he? More on that later.) Wallace LaBaw stated that Pollock's structure was built as an office, not a home-turned-office. He described a sudden need for a Breckenridge records repository. According to LaBaw, the erection of a rough log building on the

This photograph, probably taken in 1868 or 1869, shows William Pollock's North Main Street log cabin on the north (right) and the National Saloon on the south. The sign above the cabin door reads "Recorder's Office." By 1869, a hotel occupied the former saloon. From July 1876 through February 1888 the original saloon housed county offices. By 1896 that same structure became the first Occidental Hotel. In 1902 the Our House lodging establishment replaced the hotel. Note the stuffed wild cat on the cabin porch; most likely it is part of Edwin Carter's vast taxidermy collection. Possibly the man behind the cat is that "log-cabin naturalist," Carter. Photo courtesy of Maureen Nicholls.

west side of Main Street in 1862 met that need. The office still occupied a log cabin in 1866.

✦ Masonic Hall

The first courthouse had a one-month residence in Breckenridge's original Masonic Hall. The Hall was located above a furniture store near the corner of Lincoln Avenue and Main Street. That second story also held county offices and meeting rooms. Sandra F. Pritchard, Ph.D., in *Roadside Summit, Part II: The Human Landscape,* states that after its short life in the Masonic Hall, the county moved the courthouse to the Park Hotel *in Breckenridge.*

Where did they go?

Not only did governmental offices move, so did the Masonic Hall, to the second floor of M.D. Miller's building on the east side of Main Street between Adams and Washington streets. The Masons' third and last move was to a building built in 1892 for Dr. B.A. "Braz" Arbogast on the east side of South Main Street at the Washington Street intersection.*

The Arbogast Building originally housed Frank T. Patten's mercantile, Patten's Place II, on the first floor and Arbogast's medical practice on the second. After renting the upstairs for a while, in 1906 the Masons purchased the entire structure for $800 from county physician Arbogast, who was also county coroner and county superintendent of schools.

Pritchard's reference to the Breckenridge Park Hotel poses a mystery. Yes, the BOCC did appropriate $125 for the purchase of the Park Hotel. But in May 1862, Parkville was the county seat, and that's where the county meetings were

---

* One source puts the date of the Arbogast Building as 1894.

held. If a hotel in any town other than Parkville were purchased to be used as a courthouse, its location likely would
have been noted in the records.

✦ Rankin Building
The first official house of records and courts following the
log cabin on the Enterline King Store property was in the
Rankin building, north of the *Journal* office.*

Whatever building served as the courthouse in 1866, it
doubled, for a while that year, as the home of "Marshel" and
Agnes Silverthorn. The Aug. 25, 1866 BOCC meeting minutes
show that the couple was ordered to pay $15 "for use of the
courthouse while occupying same."

At their July 13, 1868 meeting, the commissioners ordered that notices be posted for the letting of a contract to repair and reframe the courthouse. Two weeks later they authorized county commissioner Charles Donnelly to procure a suitable place at a reasonable price in which to hold court until
the courthouse was repaired. Donnelly must have secured a
room in the Silverthorn Hotel, for on June 4, 1870, Agnes Silverthorn requested $25 "for using her building as a courtroom"
during 1869. The landlady eventually settled for $15.

Shortly after the renovation order and the stay with the
Silverthorns, the commissioners decided to demolish their
courthouse structure. Either the courthouse repair job was
shoddy and short-lived or the old growing pains reemerged, for
the commissioners agreed, at their June 1, 1872 meeting, to
tear down the structure. They ordered the sale of the building's

---

* The Rankin building was operated as a hotel by 1869 if not before. By 1896, the building
  was home to the first Occidental Hotel. Other sources place James Rankin's hotel two doors
  south of the *Journal* office in an 1866 structure that became, in 1898, widow Mary Kane's
  boardinghouse.

logs to the highest bidder able to pay cash within 10 days. At the same meeting, the commissioners approved the request for new courthouse construction proposals "according to the plans and specifications in the hands of the county clerk."

Again their plans fizzled. No building activity took place. No proposals were recorded in the county minutes. Most likely court continued to be held in a Silverthorn Hotel room.

By 1876 space for county offices as well as for a courtroom was needed. At their July 6, 1876 meeting, the commissioners approved the rental of the Rankin House for county offices at $10 a month. Rent payments to James and Lucinda Rankin continued for 12 years, through February 1888.

The Rankin place originally housed the National Saloon. By 1869 it was a lodging establishment. After it housed the county offices it was used as a dwelling. In 1896 it became the first Occidental Hotel; in 1902 it was renamed Our House. The second Occidental Hotel was built south of its namesake.

The Silverthorn Hotel proprietors never lost their desire to house the county courthouse in their building. Marshall Silverthorn sent a communication to the BOCC requesting the rental of his hotel for that purpose. Mention of his letter was entered into the minutes of the Jan. 7, 1878 meeting. The commissioners took no action on his application, preferring to wait until a full board was seated. Six months later they still had not addressed his application!

In the then-typical verbose way of county clerks, the minutes of the Jan. 11, 1888 meeting state that "on account of the poor condition of the county clerk's office and want of more protection for county records, the board thought it advisable to make a change in the different county offices to have the records more secure and a building more fitted for the offices." The board charged Commissioner Robert W. Foote with obtaining a one-year lease on the former Bank of Breckenridge building on Ridge Street from Job A. Cooper, with the "privilege" of extending the lease for a second year at the same fee.

The $40-a-month lease negotiated by Foote was approved by the BOCC at its March 5, 1888 meeting. Foote delivered the lease to county clerk William F. Forman on Feb. 28, 1888, with the expectation that all offices would move into their new spaces by March 1 so the county wouldn't "hold possession of both buildings at the beginning of the month." (Hope 1888 was a leap year!) "Both" refers to the bank building and to the Rankin House. The clerk, on Feb. 28, was ordered to inform Lucinda Rankin of the move, in effect giving the landlady no notice of a pending vacancy.

Foote, responsible for assigning rooms to the various county officials, gave the county clerk the downstairs front room and vault; the clerk shared the front of his office with the district clerk. The sheriff was assigned the first room to the left on the upper floor, while the county judge had the front room on the upper floor.

For some reason the treasurer didn't want to work in the same building as the other county officials. He requested and was granted approval to house his office opposite the bank in a building formerly occupied by Peterbaugh and Bullis. So badly did the treasurer want that space that he offered to pay the rent and to furnish the room at his own expense!

> ### A permanent home? Don't bank on it!
>
> The bank building, built in 1880 for $3,000, originally housed the Bank of Breckenridge. It opened for business on May 20, 1880, with a working capital of $30,000. Despite the bank's amenities -- a $3,600 first-class vault and a five-ton safe -- it folded in 1886. George and Peter Engle purchased the failing bank and reopened it as the Engle Brothers Exchange Bank in 1888. County offices shared space with the bank in 1888 and 1889.

County Seat Competition Heats Up

Perhaps the commissioners' lethargy gave opportunity to more energetic officials in Frisco and Dillon, who in the early 1880s began an effort to relocate the county seat. Had the rival towns' efforts proved successful, all the time spent on shuffling county offices would have been wasted.

Dillon and Frisco attempted to wrest away the county-seat designation from Breckenridge in 1882 through a county-wide election. At a special BOCC meeting on Oct. 4, 1882, Summit County citizens presented the county commissioners with a petition asking for a vote on moving the seat of government from Breckenridge to Frisco.

James R. Oliver, in his Oct. 7, 1882 *Montezuma Mill-run* editorial, threw his support behind Frisco. (Dillon hadn't entered the field at the time of Oliver's editorial. Had it been a candidate then, Oliver would have embraced Dillon as his first choice.) The editor's eloquent words weren't persuasive enough, however: of 2,128 votes cast, 1,011 favored moving the seat to Dillon, 832 wanted to keep the seat in Breckenridge and only 285 supported Frisco as the seat of government.

The lack of support for Frisco must have come as quite a surprise to its town fathers who had, more than a year earlier, reserved a town lot for a future Summit County courthouse. Since the two-thirds majority vote required to move the county seat failed, Breckenridge's status remained intact.

The *Summit County Leader* anticipated that Dillon would enter into a second county-seat fray by the autumn of 1888. In a March 3, 1888 article, the newspaper alerted readers to the likelihood of another government-seat contest. The *Leader* raised the possibility that 200 or 300 transient railroad voters could swing a challenge in Dillon's favor, even though a majority of "actual and permanent" residents cast ayes for Breckenridge.

Despite the county-seat challenge, the commissioners in Breckenridge continued to play hopscotch with county offices. And no matter where the county moved its offices, some dissatisfied citizens soon voiced their disapproval. On Oct. 7, 1889, Board of Trade members Charles A. Finding, Edward Radigan, W.A. Potter and J.C. Fincher appeared before the BOCC asking that $2,000 be set aside to repair the county-owned buildings on Main Street "to make them suitable for courthouse and county offices."

Three days later the board ordered an appropriation not to exceed $2,000 to repair the county-owned New York Store building "to make it suitable for county offices and to construct same into a courthouse." It appointed a committee of three to have plans and specifications drawn, to advertise for bids and to award the contract. That same day the BOCC ordered that district court be held in Fireman's Hall for the October term at a daily rental of $5.

Thus at the end of 1889, the county moved most of its offices to the east side of South Main Street, just south of the justice office. The 1890, 1892, 1896, 1900 and 1902 maps of Breckenridge verify this, showing three adjacent buildings housing county offices on the east side of South Main Street near the Lincoln Avenue intersection. From north to south, those offices were the county offices, the courthouse and the sheriff's office. The 1890, 1892 and 1896 maps also show one county office on the west side of North Main Street. That building is not included in the 1900 or 1902 maps.

An idea before its time

J.C. Fincher's appearance at the BOCC meeting shouldn't have come as a surprise to the commissioners. In a Jan. 14, 1888 editorial in the *Summit County Journal*, he raged about the "absolutely disgraceful absence of a county building .... unsafe condition of the records .... inconvenience ensuing from the scattered offices of the various officials .... that should no longer be tolerated." Fincher suggested that the county consolidate its offices and build its own courthouse. The removal of the Fireman's Hall had left county-deeded land vacant. There the county could erect a courthouse to accommodate district and county courtrooms, a jail and offices for the clerk and recorder, district clerk, treasurer, surveyor and commissioners. Twenty years later his vision became reality.

The county buildings seemed to be victims of the same planned obsolescence built into today's appliances. By July 12, 1890, less than a year after the $2,000 repair and construction job, the BOCC found it necessary to appropriate $998 more for repairs to the same building. Those repairs did the trick; the next "fix" wasn't needed until July 17, 1895, five years later. At that time the commissioners ordered repairs to the courthouse.

The job, contracted to William McAdoo, came to $28 for lumber and labor.

You get what you pay for, and for $28 the commissioners got less than a year's worth of repair. Thus on April 10, 1896, the board advertised in the *Summit County Journal* for bids for putting new roofs on the sheriff's and recorder's offices, repairing the courtroom roof, papering and painting all office interiors, and adding two coats of paint on the front of office exteriors. Eli Fletcher was awarded the contract for his low bid of $430. Fletcher worked fast and well. The BOCC examined the repairs on July 8 and declared them satisfactory.

All the repair work on the county buildings must have made the commissioners acutely aware of the expenses of owning and maintaining structures. Worse than repair cost, however, was total replacement cost. To protect the county from such dire potential expense, the commissioners, at their June 2, 1898 meeting, ordered the purchase of $2,000 worth of insurance on the buildings.

By April 1900, the county buildings bulged at their seams. On April 5, the commissioners instructed county clerk Forman to advertise for bids for construction of a commissioners' room adjacent to the clerk's office. Called an annex, room specifications included dimensions of 10' x 14'; a 9' ceiling; double-boarded walls on the east and south sides; interior sealed with rough native lumber; two 12" x 14" windows; one door, and a floor of Texas pine. The annex contract was awarded to J.A. Stephens at the May 12, 1900 BOCC meeting.

Two months later, on July 7, 1900, the commissioners ordered that the clerk's office be updated by installing a water connection. They awarded the contract to dig a ditch to J.R.

Three county buildings anchor the east side of South Main Street near the intersection with Lincoln Avenue. The building at the far left housed the offices of the clerk and the treasurer. The middle structure served as the courthouse. On the right is the Galloway Building where the sheriff had his office. The two northernmost structures (left) were totally destroyed by fire on July 7, 1936.

25

Adams, and approved C.A. Finding's low bid to supply the pipes and fittings.

Shedding a little light on the subject

The county jumped on the electricity bandwagon quite soon after lights appeared in Breckenridge. At its Jan. 12, 1892 meeting, the BOCC ordered county commissioner M.H. Huntress to "look after the lighting of the county offices with electricity." Huntress was given full power to act. Any contract he negotiated with the utility company was to be ratified and approved by the board at its April meeting.

And so, on April 5, 1892, the board approved the installation of 13 lights by the Breckenridge Electric Light Company. Four lights were to go in the county courtroom; three in the county clerk's office; two in the treasurer's office, and one each in the sheriff's office, the school superintendent's office, the district clerk's office and the district clerk's vault.

Each light cost $3 to install. Monthly cost for all lights except those in the courtroom was $7. The courtroom electricity cost $.05 per light per night when used.

At its Dec. 3, 1901 meeting, the board voted to switch the county's electricity account to the Goldpan Engineering Mine and Supply Company as of Jan. 1, 1902. Its quarterly price for 39 16-candle-power lights was $25, nearly half of what the Breckenridge Electric Light Company charged. Despite the agreed-upon $25 fee, however, over a 3-year period the county averaged $33.26 a quarter.

The 39 lights were scattered around Breckenridge in numerous county buildings. Four were in the hospital, one in the jail, nine in the courtroom, one in the wood shed, one in the upstairs hall and 24 in the various offices (treasurer, six; assessor, six; sheriff, two, and clerk, ten).

The 1896 courtroom roof repair needed its own repair by mid-1901. The commissioners, at their July 9, 1901 meeting, instructed county attorney William A. Guyselman to draw plans and specifications for a "new, good and substantial roof" over the building, commonly called the courtroom, used by the district and county judges.

The commissioners examined Guyselman's plans, found them acceptable, paid the attorney $26 for his services and ordered county clerk Forman to advertise in the *Summit County Journal* and the *Breckenridge Bulletin* for bids to install a new roof. Eli Fletcher, who submitted the lowest bid, was awarded the contract. One year later, in July 1902, Fletcher was back in the courtroom making additional repairs, followed by Henry York in October. Less than a year later, in July 1903, the BOCC hired William McAdoo to make more renovations. The county buildings must have resembled patchwork quilts!

A repairless 2½-year period occurred between July 1903 and October 1905. That was followed by the installation of a screen door on the courthouse and repairs to the treasurer's office. The patchwork quilt took on an even busier appearance.

Pyrotechs needn't apply

The old courthouse on South Main Street contained a two-story brick vault. A raging fire on July 7, 1936, left only that vault intact. Also totally destroyed by the blaze were the two-story building in which the county clerk's and treasurer's offices had been located and the unoccupied Galloway Building that had, years earlier, housed the county sheriff's office. In 1936, these old county buildings were part of the Forman Estate.

The July 7, 1936 fire began in the vacant county courthouse, the tall structure with the false front. Directly north (left) of the courthouse were the offices of the county clerk and county treasurer, which the fire also demolished. The blaze ate its way through those offices and continued north to devour the neighboring Summit Drug Store and The Shoe Shop (formerly a dance hall and saloon) at the corner of South Main Street and Lincoln Avenue.

This hearse, most likely driven by a local character named Buttons, was one of many vehicles in Breckenridge's annual No Man's Land parade. Behind the hearse is the two-story brick vault that survived the July 7, 1936 fire. To the right of the vault is the Galloway Building. The hearse, built in the 1890s for $3,000, was first owned by Huntress and Rogers. Later owners included Jeanette Gough and Harold Minowitz. Minowitz displayed the hearse, claimed to be the oldest in Colorado, in a separate building on the Wildwood Lodge property in Old Dillon.

At the time of the fire the county relief office used the clerk's office for storage and for dispensing foods and materials. Fortunately, canned goods, kept locked in the vault, were spared from damage.

Mack Osborne saw the blaze from his house and turned in the fire alarm at 3:50 a.m. The brick vault in the courthouse and the fire wall on the Kaiser store slowed the path of the flames to such an extent that the Breckenridge Volunteer Fire Department could stop their spread and limit their destruction. Nevertheless, losses from the fire were devastating since none of the businesses was insured.*

Two boys playing with firecrackers left over from the Fourth of July fireworks display apparently caused the fire. Since that incident, town officials have banned fireworks in Breckenridge.

Mysteries #3 and #4: First County Clerk
Whodunit? County Clerk Thatcher is prime suspect.

The mystery of Summit County's early history continues to deepen. The puzzles this time are two. First is the identity of the first county clerk and recorder. Second is the identity of the clerk whose attempt to return the county records to Parkville was aborted.

First: Many historians promote William P. Pollock as the first Summit County clerk and recorder. Indeed, the sign over the door of Rankin's former Our House on North Main Street supports that contention.

---

* Decades after the fire, Breckenridge Land, Inc. (BLI) bought the property with the vault. When BLI built the Breckenridge Inn (now the Breckenridge Mountain Lodge) at the south end of town, bricks from the vault were used for the lobby floor. The floor was so uneven, however, that the bricks were later removed.

Official county records, however, dispute the sign's wording. Not only was Pollock not the first county clerk, he didn't even make the First Four list. According to those county records, Joseph Thatcher, on Dec. 2, 1861, was elected to a two-year term as county clerk. D. G. Peabody, BOCC clerk (and county clerk), signed Thatcher's certificate of election.

More than likely, Peabody was the first county clerk, although he may have been appointed rather than elected to the position. Thatcher may have been the first elected county clerk. Thatcher started filing and recording on Dec. 22, 1861, and began attesting on Jan. 6, 1862.

Thatcher's name no longer appeared on county documents after Jan. 1, 1863. Instead, Olophant B. Brown, a deputy county clerk and recorder as well as county treasurer, attested, filed and recorded the official documents. County clerk by Feb. 9, 1863, Brown lasted one and a half years. W.E. Grinnell took over Brown's position on Aug. 13, 1864.

Other than serving as an election judge and an election clerk, William P. Pollock wasn't mentioned in county records until June 7, 1864, when he witnessed the recording of five mining claims. The claims were filed and recorded by Grinnell and his deputy, William Corning. Pollock's name first appeared on documents as deputy recorder under Grinnell on Aug. 23, 1864. His term didn't last long: J.A. Christian replaced him a month later, on Sept. 24, 1864. Pollock's name appeared for the first time as Summit County recorder on Sept. 15, 1865, in a mining lode-record book.* James Willoughby followed him on Oct. 3, 1871.

* Pollock's name appeared as recorder in a pre-exemption water-claims book on Sept. 18, 1865. He continued as county recorder until Sept. 18, 1871. Records show Pollock attesting as county clerk on June 7, 1869, July 5, 1870 and July 5, 1871 and as clerk of the BOCC from Oct. 21, 1865 to July 5, 1871.

Barely visible, the words on this building's weathered sign state that William Pollock was the county's first clerk and recorder in 1862 and that this structure housed his office. The author believes that Pollock's log-cabin office occupied space two lots north of this site. History buffs can view this enlarged and re-sided structure at 115 North Main Street in Breckenridge. The south (left) wing is still connected to the building; the north wing met its demise years ago.

For whatever reason, the earliest county clerks held their positions, on average, less than a year. Pollock, once elected, broke the pattern; he lasted six years. Maybe that's why some historians consider him the first county clerk.

What's this? Dereliction of duty?

Unlike many of their contemporaries, former county clerks Pollock and Willoughby stayed in Summit County for decades. Pollock served as an election judge from the Recen Precinct six times between 1875 and 1885. Appointed county assessor on July 6, 1874, he held that position through 1875. Ten years later, he was appointed county assessor for 1886 and he was reappointed for 1887. Willoughby was deputy county assessor in 1884 and 1886.

Pollock resigned as assessor on April 4, 1887. Presumably Willoughby was not reappointed for 1887. The duo's reputation was publicly tarnished on July 8, 1887, when the BOCC decided that as the assessor and deputy assessor, Pollock and Willoughby failed to do their duty in 1886. The board further determined that the men had been paid all that they were entitled to "as the negligence of the duties caused the different county officers much trouble and put the county to considerable unnecessary expense."

In a final act, the commissioners, on Oct. 8, 1886, disallowed payment of the bills presented by Pollock and Willoughby, nine months after the two sought appropriation for same. Sometimes the wheels of government moved so slowly they n-e-a-r-l-y s-t-o-p—p—e—d.

The BOCC decision censuring the two men sounds firm enough. Nevertheless, on Oct. 3, 1887, the commissioners selected Willoughby as an election judge from Lincoln Precinct #2. Perhaps the candidate pool was very small. Perhaps the prevailing philosophy was "let bygones be bygones"....

People note that you can't believe everything you read. Usually that means that you shouldn't count on newspapers for accuracy. In this case, however, skepticism should apply to the sign above the door to the former Our House which reads "Office of Wm. Pollock, 1862, First Clerk and Recorder, Summit County." Aside from the fact that the sign is on the wrong building, the sign should read "Office of Wm. Pollock, *1865*, *Fifth* Clerk and Recorder, Summit County." The information is so full of errors that it's downright .... mysterious.*

Winning is in the eye of the beholder

The new county made election of officers one of its first official acts. At least one election winner viewed his popularity as a hardship: the newly-elected assessor declined to serve, presumably out of fear that miners would not take kindly to being assessed.

Who should arrive in the area in the spring of 1862 but Father John Lewis Dyer. It is doubtful that anyone embraced the man of the cloth more than the unhappy assessor, who successfully implored the good preacher to serve as deputy county assessor. Although he initially declined, Father Dyer eventually agreed to take the position. Thus the now-famous "snowshoe itinerant" made the first official property assessments in Summit County.

Two years elapsed between the time Father Dyer submitted the $50 charge for his services and the time he received payment, despite the fact that abundant placer gold was discovered in nearby gulches during that period. The wheels of government turned slowly even then.

* Robin Theobald, son of the present owner of Rankin's former Our House, said it's possible the sign above the door was made and erected by the U.S. Forest Service years after Pollock's term in office. Others say it was erected in time for the Rush for Rockies celebration in 1959. While this building housed the county offices for 12 years, the author doesn't believe that Pollock ever worked in it. His office was two lots north in a log cabin.

The Rev. Father John Lewis Dyer, a man for all seasons: ordained minister, prospector, maker of fine snowshoes [skis], mail carrier, builder, Colorado State Senate chaplain, deputy county assessor. A reluctant deputy assessor, Father Dyer made the first official property assessments in Summit County.

Back to Mystery #4: Which county clerk attempted to steal the county records from the Silverthorn Hotel and return them to Parkville, only to be thwarted by Mrs. Silverthorn? Assuming this attempt occurred in 1862, the year of the first and successful heist, the finger of guilt points to Joseph Thatcher, county clerk from Dec. 12, 1861, to Jan. 1, 1863.

One theory to support Thatcher's guilt is that, as an officer of the Masonic Lodge, he knew the Society needed money. Renting out space in its Parkville Hall to the county enabled the organization to raise essential funds and alleviate some of its financial problems. Of course, if the county seat were in Breckenridge, the BOCC would have no reason to rent a hall in Parkville, so presumably the clerk took it upon himself to return the seat of government to its original location.

Having unraveled these threads of "mystery history," the courthouse story now shifts to a momentous few years after the turn of the century. Then the long-held dream of a large and beautiful courthouse for Summit County finally saw its reality.

Chapter Two

The People Demand a New Courthouse

By 1908, the Summit County community, tired of having its county offices hopscotch all over Breckenridge, demanded erection of a new and proper courthouse. The citizens pressed the commissioners to replace the existing offices labeled as "inadequate, unsuitable and in bad condition." On Sept. 3, 1908, 115 county taxpayers petitioned the county commissioners to "enter an order of record specifying the amount required for the purpose of building a new courthouse" .... and to "submit the question to a vote of the people .... at the next general election."

The commissioners acted immediately. At that Sept. 3 meeting, Chairman A.W. Phillips moved that the question of a $75,000 indebtedness to erect, equip and furnish a courthouse be put before the county's legal voters at the Nov. 3, 1908 election. He also proposed that notice of the election be posted in a conspicuous place in each voting precinct at least 30 days prior to the election. The motions passed, 2-1.

At the Nov. 3, 1908 election, a majority of the voters cast their ballots in favor of creating a bonded indebtedness to build a new courthouse. That indebtedness had a $75,000 cap. A citizen committee, assigned to find the most beautiful spot in Breckenridge, identified the north side of Lincoln Avenue between Ridge and French streets as the site for the new courthouse. The property enjoyed morning sunlight and a height sufficient to overlook the rest of the town. Three architectural parties submitted plans and specifications for the courthouse.

From those three, the commissioners selected John James Huddart to design the project. They hired Ladd Sanger Contracting Company to build it.

The site for the new courthouse (208 Lincoln Avenue) measured 192 feet on Lincoln Avenue, 151 feet on French Street and 150 feet on Ridge Street. The site's previous occupants included a cigar-manufacturing factory owned by George Siebe, the Fireman's Hall (now the parking lot), George and Peter Engle's billiard saloon (which was moved to a different location on Lincoln Avenue) and the Congregational Church.

Moving buildings was as common as moving furniture

The courthouse property shows Breckenridge's propensity to move its buildings. The Fireman's Hall, built in July 1880, was moved from the Lincoln Avenue site to the east side of Main Street in January 1888. The Work Projects Administration (WPA) demolished that hall and the town hall in 1941. Lumber salvaged from the razing was used in the construction of a new town hall/firehouse on the west side of Main Street.

The Congregational Church had a short existence at the pre-courthouse site. Its first service there was held on Oct. 30, 1881; by September 1882 the church was moved to the east side of Harris Street between Lincoln and Washington avenues. The Episcopalian Church, which since July 1887 had used the Congregational facility for many of its services, purchased the building on Nov. 28, 1891. That sale marked the disbanding of the Congregational Church in Breckenridge.

The Cornerstone Is Laid to Rest

The county wasted no time in tackling the massive construction project. After selecting the site, architect and contractor, work moved at a rapid pace. The first of two elaborate ceremonies celebrating the building took place less than nine months after voters cast their ayes for a new courthouse.

A big crowd watched the Masons set the cornerstone in the southwest corner of the building at 3:30 p.m. on Saturday, July 31, 1909. All businesses suspended operations for the afternoon so everyone could attend. Banners and streamers hung across all the streets in the lavishly-decorated town. Breckenridge residents had been encouraged to decorate their homes and businesses with the "national colors" as well.

Grand Masons and other dignitaries arrived by train from Fairplay, Alma, Como and Jefferson. Local firemen under the command of Chief Knorr, 75 Masons in regalia and a brass band marched in a parade behind Masonic grand officers riding in two large Kingsbury autos. A chorus of 50 voices, led by J.H. Von Thun, added their joyous sounds during the festivities.

The grand officers of the order of Ancient Free and Accepted Masons "squared and plumbed" the granite cornerstone. In the center of the cornerstone they deposited a copper box that contained the following: a copy of the resolution passed by the county commissioners authorizing the construction of the courthouse; samples of town and county bond issues; then-current coins; copies of local papers; gold nuggets; literature pertaining to the county; *Sweet Summer Land*, an idyl written in 1886 by Florence Watson and published in

Looking like a column of dominoes, 75 Masons wearing their distinctive aprons march east on Lincoln Avenue between Main and Ridge Streets in Breckenridge. They paraded to the July 31, 1909 cornerstone-laying ceremony for the new courthouse.

1892 by the Chain and Hardy Co. of Denver; and a copy of the constitution and by-laws of Blue River Lodge No. 47 A.F. and A.M. Before laying the copper box in cement, the Grand Master mixed a quantity of gold into the mortar. The stone was then "sealed with the wine, the corn and the oil."

The inscriptions on the cornerstone are on its west and south sides. The west-side inscription reads: "Laid by the M.W. Grand Lodge A.F. & A.M. of Colorado. A.D. 1909. A.L. 5909." The wording on the south side is: "Erected A.D. 1909. County Commissioners A.W. Phillips, B.F. Rice, W.H. Hampton. John J. Huddart, Architect."* Everything was perfect except that Mr. Hampton's initials were transposed in the cutting of the stone. The mistake was later rectified, but noticeably so.

After laying the cornerstone, the Hon. H.H. Eddy, former state senator from Chihuahua in Summit County's Peru Creek Valley, gave a 25-minute speech. The singing of *America* and a lengthy address by District and County Attorney J.T. "Sunny Jim" Hogan followed Eddy's presentation. The Hon. C.L. Westerman, scheduled to give a 10- to 20-minute speech on Summit County's mineral resources, begged to be excused owing to the lateness of the hour.

The evening of July 31, 1909, saw a banquet for the Masons and their wives and county and town officers and their spouses. The festivities concluded with a magnificent free ball at the Grand Army of the Republic Hall on the east side of North Main Street, across the street from the former county offices.

---

* Denver architect John James Huddart designed the standard plan adopted by many armories around the state.

In full regalia, officers of the Grand Lodge of Ancient Free and Accepted Masons of the State of Colorado laid the Summit County Courthouse cornerstone. The Summit County Journal referred to these grand officers as Master Masons. The Father Dyer United Methodist Church, on the right in back, has since been moved to Wellington Avenue where it was later enlarged.

Original Features and Architectural Details

The new Summit County Courthouse earned the community's pride. It was a fine building, both inside and out. Its special features and details included:

+ Colonial-Revival style architecture.
+ Red pressed-brick exterior; brick indicated a building's importance.
+ Tan sandstone and green/tan brick trim.
+ Four-sided cupola above two pediments.
+ North and south entry pediments that feature painted mining (south) and railroading (north) scenes in bas-relief on pressed zinc.
+ Hipped gable roof.
+ Pedimented entry bays.
+ Balanced fenestration (paired sashed windows on all four sides).
+ Miniature concrete pilasters set into the brick just below the architrave.
+ Large, octagonal main-floor hall.
+ Magnificent interior golden-oak stairwell and woodwork.
+ High pressed-tin ceiling.
+ Chandeliers.
+ Two vaults -- a three-story one on the west side and a two-story one on the east side.
+ Courtrooms on the upper floor; offices for elected officials on the middle floor; restrooms, apartment and jail in the basement, peephole and all.
+ Concrete basement walls.

J.W. Swisher, one of the trio of bigwigs in charge of the courthouse dedication ceremony, made the opening remarks at the evening gala. An early-day resident of Montezuma, he was the last publisher of the Montezuma Millrun *(1888). Later Swisher moved to Breckenridge and published the* Breckenridge Journal *until his death more than a decade later.*

A "Necessary" Is Necessary

A restroom for women was not part of the original plan. However, some "public-spirited matrons," led by Gertrude Susan Briggle Engle, decided that the building should have a place "whither ladies .... may retire for a little privacy or rest, and where they may find the essential means of 'touching up' their complexions and rectifying possible defections of the toilet." When the group conferred with the county commissioners, they were told that the large basement room in the southeast corner of the new courthouse would be placed at their disposal.

At a meeting held at 2:30 p.m. Saturday, Feb. 12, 1910, interested ladies formulated plans for properly furnishing and decorating the room and for establishing the ways and means to garner the money for this undertaking. Exactly one month later on March 12, at a meeting in the home of the Rest-Room Association's president, Mrs. J.F. Condon, members learned that the amount required to "furnish the room in a manner befitting the name -- a rest-room" -- was estimated to be $125.

Support for the restroom had wider appeal than just from area matrons. A front-page story in the March 12, 1910 *Summit County Journal* ended with this poem:

> *They are bound to have a rest-room,*
> *Why, of course, they'll have a rest-room.*
> *That is what the smiling ladies state.*
> *Every one will do her duty --*
> *It is sure to be a beauty,*
> *For Breckenridge is always up to date.*

It didn't take long to raise the funding. Most of the furnishings, including curtains, rockers, easy chairs, a couch, carpeting and a library table, were purchased, but there were donations as well, most notably an organ from Gertrude Engle.

The Courthouse Dedication: What a Party!

From its inception, the courthouse dedication was a guaranteed hit. The overall committee, comprised of J.W. Swisher, William H. Briggle and George E. Moon, had the power to appoint subcommittees, and appoint they did. The result was a three-member finance subcommittee, a three-member refreshments subcommittee, a six-member music subcommittee and a *70-member* reception subcommittee! The latter subcommittee's membership list read like a county-wide *Who's Who*. With all of the local "Social Register" types serving on subcommittees, the ceremony was a certain success.

In a front-page article, the March 12, 1910 *Summit County Journal* urged residents to "turn out and make the occasion one of interest and pleasure." The newspaper referred to earlier days when the county seat was unstable. The article noted that the new courthouse provided "a security for the records that has been wanting ever since the county was formed, and the records will never have to be guessed at or litigated over."

The courthouse was dedicated at 8 p.m. on St. Patrick's Day, Thursday, March 17, 1910, amid an array of beautiful flowers and a flood of light from the basement to the dome. The Breckenridge Brass Band crowded into the dome and played music from that lofty height. The Hon. J.W. Swisher,

The Summit County Courthouse lobby was festooned with ribbons for its dedication. Note the numerous shiny brass spittoons strategically placed close together along the walls. The double-glass door and transom window allow plenty of light to flood the foyer.

surrounded by schoolchildren holding tiny flags, made the opening remarks. *The Star-Spangled Banner,* sung by the children, followed, and then the Rev. C.E. Snowden offered a prayer.

The band played another selection; the chairman of the meeting, county commissioner A.W. Phillips, spoke; the Breckenridge Male Quartet filled the air with song; the Hon. Caesar A. Roberts of Denver, the main speaker, addressed the crowd; the Breckenridge Orchestra played; the Rev. Snowden spoke again; the Hon. C.L. Westerman gave a talk on the mineral resources of Summit County (the speech he originally planned to make at the cornerstone-laying ceremony), and the children provided the finale -- their delightful rendition of *America.* Following the program, everyone enjoyed some punch.

Two days after the dedication, *The Summit County Journal* reported that the building "as it stands, without anything connected to it," had cost $39,215.25. Additional expenses were $2,000 for land, $600 for electrical fixtures and $1,300 for furniture, for a total of $43,115.25. The building came in significantly under the $75,000 budgeted. Despite its low cost, the community got more than it bargained for: it got a handsome structure plus a heavy infusion of community pride.

Colorful ribbons decorated the lobby of the Summit County Court-house for its dedication. Note the sign on the door to the left of the beautiful golden-oak stairway that reads "COMMISSIONERS." That door now leads to the clerk and recorder's office.

Built in 1880, the building above originally housed the Bank of Breckenridge, which folded in 1886. The Engle brothers purchased the failing bank and reopened it as the Engle Bro's Exchange Bank in 1888. The Engles brought the man on the right, William H. Briggle, to Breckenridge from Ohio to be the bank's head cashier. Briggle ran for county treasurer in 1906, but was defeated. At the time of his death in October 1924, he was a county commissioner. Briggle was one of the chairmen of the courthouse dedication party.

Chapter Three

The Courthouse Prior to Renovations

The cupola at the top of the courthouse commands an impressive view from its four sides. Since the beginning, county commissioners and some elected officials have carved their initials in the tower's soft wood.

Monitors aren't just in school hallways

Civil Defense volunteers once manned the cupola to monitor airplane activity in the Breckenridge skies. Courthouse staffers discovered, on the counter in the cupola, a log book dating back to the pre-radar 1950s that contained notations from members of the Ground Observer Corps, a branch of the Civil Defense System.

Corps members watched for airplanes, logged any and all noted aircraft in the book, and notified the State Civil Defense whenever one flew overhead. That strategic effort ended some time ago. Now the only equipment in the cupola is a partially disassembled microwave antenna.

Below the cupola, on the top floor of the courthouse, use of the rooms related to court affairs. The largest room, the one in the northeast corner, was the district courtroom. A wooden railing divided the room; it ran between the two doors on the west side of the room to the east side of the room. On the north side of the railing sat the audience and everyone else except the judge, jury and attorneys.

The district courtroom featured a pressed-tin ceiling, oak trim and "clusters of globes" for lighting. It also provided several oh-so-necessary spittoons. Two are visible in this photo -- one to the right of the open door and one behind a wooden chair to the right of the judge's leather chair.

The eight windows and the doors in the room are original. Except for one, so are all of the chandeliers (called clusters of globes by the *Summit County Journal*). The room's corners sport original vents to the attic. The pressed-tin ceiling is original also.

The judge sat on the south side of the railing in a very high seat between two original light fixtures that today flank a large map. The jury sat on chairs underneath the windows. On the outer sides of the light fixtures are doors; the door on the left (east) led to the jury deliberation room/law library, the door on the right (west) to a hallway across from which was the judge's cloak/changing room. In between the two rooms was the bailiff's room, used by attorneys as a conference room.

Next to the cloak room was the district judge's room, now the BOCC Small Conference Room. The judge had his own bathroom; its installation occasionally, but erroneously, is attributed to the first female county court judge, Jewel Smith-Biddle. Such attribution implies that the judge demanded special treatment because of her gender, but the "convenience" actually was put in prior to her early-1980's tenure.

Do as I say, not as I do

Judge Jewel Smith-Biddle was so widely known for her tough stance on drunk driving that she was nicknamed the DUI hanging judge. Ironically, she herself was charged with driving under the influence. Unlike the stiff sentences she handed down to offenders of the same crime, Smith-Biddle received only a slap on the wrist before being released on her own recognizance. Publicity about the matter was hushed to the extent possible. Such double standards were the norm two decades ago.

Judge Smith-Biddle also was known for her changing courtroom attire: purportedly she wore a red robe when she was in a bad mood (people who regularly dealt with her learned to tread cautiously then) and donned a black robe when her mood was improved. It was not unusual for a robe – of either color – to cover a warm-up suit.

Next to the judge's quarters was a court clerk area. The area formed an L, and much of its space was taken up by a large counter and by the district court safe. (The space is now occupied by an elevator shaft and the county court safe.) The court clerk area also served as the lunchroom. At the north end of the area was the county courtroom, and next to that was an attorney conference room.

On the main floor, the county clerk and recorder's office occupied most of the west side; the north end of that office housed the clerk-operated motor vehicle department. Behind the clerk's office was the BOCC Meeting Room. The north end of the main floor's east side was home to the assessor's office; south of that was the treasurer's office.

The basement housed a one-cell jail, an apartment, two vaults, the boiler room (in the northeast corner – it contained the coal furnace and coal chute) and the men's and women's restrooms. A peephole on the northwest side of the basement lobby allowed caretakers to view the jail cell without going into the jail.

The courthouse's single cell wasn't the first jail in the county. At their May 20, 1862 meeting, at which the commissioners appropriated $125 for the Park Hotel, they also ordered the $75 purchase of a house on Lot 6, Block 3, on Colorado Street to be used as a county jail. Presumably this house was in Parkville, then the county seat. The commissioners spent a lot

Two rather austere but respectable-looking gentlemen sit in the district courtroom. They both look like they have plenty of important words to bestow upon anyone who will listen. Perhaps the bouquet of flowers on the table indicates that the occasion was more social than serious.

of money that day. In addition to buying two buildings, one for a courthouse and one for a jail, they approved the expenditure of $375 to repair the Colorado Street house to make it suitable for a jail. They put Sheriff William M. Evans in charge of the repairs.*

Eleven years later the commissioners appropriated funds again ($318.27 on Oct. 6, 1873) "for the purchase of a building erected for a jail." The procurement was made at the urging of the county sheriff, A.L. Shock.

Not in my backyard!

As early as 1877 Breckenridge had incarcerated its miscreants in its own small jail. Called a calaboose, the jail was on county property on French Street immediately north of the northwest corner of Lincoln Avenue and French Street. That lot is now part of the courthouse property.

In October 1881, Town of Breckenridge trustees contracted with J. Shidler to move the calaboose from French Street to the west end of the Lincoln Avenue Bridge, much to the dismay of nearby residents. Despite the resistance, Shidler moved the calaboose to the bridge's west end. There it remained until it was retransplanted to almost the exact spot from which it came. The calaboose's final move was into the basement of the new courthouse.

---

* Specifications for the 1862 jail were just that – specific. The floor had to be made of 10"-thick timber. A partition had to divide the structure's back room into two equal parts (cells). The outside walls were to be lined with 2"-thick planks against 10"-thick timbers that formed the walls. The ceiling was to be made of 8"-square timbers. Each cell needed a door to the front room. The doors had to be constructed of 3"-thick planks; they were to be lined on the inside with iron not less than 1/16" thick and covered on the outside with 1"-thick pine planks. The doors had to swing out into the front room.

The November 1892 map of Breckenridge shows a county jail adjacent to the town's calaboose on the block bordered by French and Ridge streets and Lincoln and Carter avenues.* By 1899, the jail had outlived its usefulness ... or had it?

A Mr. Finch from the Pauly Jail Building and Manufacturing Company of St. Louis, Missouri, appeared before the BOCC at its Oct. 3, 1899 meeting. The topic of Mr. Finch's presentation? Jail cells. Two days later, at their Oct. 5 meeting, the commissioners adopted the following resolution:

Whereas in the opinion of the Honorable Board of County Commissioners, Summit County should have a jail for the care of prisoners,

And whereas in the opinion of the board, the cost of transportation and the paying of guards for jail will in the course of a year or two cost fully as much as to build a suitable jail at Breckenridge,

And whereas the county is the owner of a suitable site in said town of Breckenridge for the erection of a jail and supplying same with two steel cells,

And whereas it is for the best interest of all taxpayers and citizens of Summit County to build and maintain a county jail,

Therefore we appropriate the sum of $3,500 for the building of a county jail and make a levy of one mill on the dollar on all taxable property for jail purposes.

---

* Carter Avenue, originally named Grant Avenue, was renamed Wellington Avenue in the 1970s.

On Oct. 7, 1899, the *Summit County Journal* praised the county commissioners for appropriating *$3,000* (lesson: question a newspaper's accuracy) to build a new jail. The newspaper hailed the tax levy of one mill for jail purposes as "a move in the right direction" in light of the "many jail breaks in the county."

That same day the BOCC instructed the county clerk to advertise for bids in the *Summit County Journal* and the *Breckenridge Bulletin*.* Bids were to be accepted until noon on Oct. 17. After the contract was awarded, the builder had less than a month -- until Nov. 10, 1899, to be exact -- to complete the structure.

The BOCC awarded the jail contract on Oct. 17, 1899, to the only bidder, Charles A. Finding. His bid was for $1,200. That same day the commissioners added a new specification: the furnishing and hanging of double-back doors. The next day they tacked on still another requirement: one-sash windows.

By Nov. 4, the double iron door and frame were in place. Soon after came was the insertion of the two steel cages inside the granite walls. Summit County would have "creditable 'rooms' in which to securely detain its criminal subjects," predicted the weekly paper.

The board examined the new jail on Jan. 2, 1900. Following the inspection the commissioners moved that the county clerk draw three warrants of $400 each "in favor of C.A. Finding in payment for jail."

* Specifications (again!) in the ad included size (20' x 20'), material (stone) and completion date (Nov. 10, 1899).

The commissioners visited the jail again on April 5, 1900. Not satisfied with what they saw, they instructed county clerk Forman, at their May 12, 1900 meeting, to advertise for bids for putting two coats of paint on the jail's woodwork and for installing a water connection to the structure. Eli Fletcher won the painting contract; C.A. Finding was awarded the contract to supply pipes and fittings, and N. Lee Bryan's low bid to dig a ditch to the jail was accepted.

The jail failed to live up to expectations. On Dec. 9, 1900, less than a year after its completion, the newspaper lamented the fact that the jail wasn't holding its prisoners. More repairs were done at the end of 1900, but they weren't secure enough to prevent jail breaks. Sheriff J.G. Detwiler submitted a bill of $4 to the county commissioners on Jan. 9, 1901, for "telegraphing for escaped prisoners Smith and Jackson."

Repairs continued to mount up. Plumbing work, done in January 1902, cost $10.02. More costly was the installation of a screen in July 1902 for $65.20.

Meanwhile, the county's old jail sat empty; county officials had no use for it. Town of Breckenridge officials thought otherwise. The town appealed to the BOCC at the latter's July 8, 1904 meeting, to be allowed to use the jail for fire-apparatus storage. The county so ordered. In return for "free rent," the town agreed to give possession of the jail back to the county at any time upon the county's demand.

A decade after the *Summit County Journal* publicized the jail's inability to hold prisoners, the problem was solved with the construction of the new courthouse. The town's old calaboose was placed in its basement.

Keeping up with the Joneses

After the courthouse was built, the Breckenridge town fathers quickly decided to modernize the county seat. Instead of the usual boardwalk, they chose a concrete sidewalk to match the courthouse's concrete walkway and steps from the street to the walkway. The sidewalk ran in front of the courthouse on Lincoln Avenue down to Main Street. From then on, boardwalks became passe, and new sidewalks in Breckenridge were concrete.

Chapter Four

The First of Many Improvements

From the beginning, the courthouse had a dual personality. Not only did people work there, but some *lived* there. Of course, the courthouse jail always housed a collection of felons, thugs and drunks. But a number of courthouse staff members also took up residence in the building.

Like the jailbirds, these guests lived rent-free. These live-ins were the custodians/handy-men who shoveled the snow, fed the boiler, looked after the inmates and did odd jobs. They resided with their families in an apartment in the northeast corner of the basement off the boiler room.

In the '40s and '50s, Russell and Anna Mumford and their two daughters lived in the apartment. Mumford, born in 1904 at Cataract Ranch in the Lower Blue Valley of Summit County, wasn't only the janitor (actually, his wife did most of the cleaning; he did the snow shoveling), he was also the county court judge (he had to get a General Education Degree to qualify for the position) and the county motor-vehicle examiner. At times Mumford acted as the county jailer as well.

Not only did a judge and his wife occupy the apartment, so did sheriffs and their wives. It was not uncommon for a sheriff's or judge's wife to make breakfast and lunch for the inmates in return for free lodging. Several custodians lived in the courthouse apartment over the years.

One of Mumford's duties was to take inmates out to dinner at either the Gold Pan Saloon, Colorado House or

Brown Hotel. A county commissioner, sheriff or assessor usually accompanied them. Such "dining out" wasn't extravagant. As long as there was only one inmate in the jail and no live-in cook on the premises, it was less expensive to carry a restaurant-made meal to the jail or to have the inmate eat at a restaurant than to employ an outside cook.

The practice of going to restaurants was common during the 1940s, '50s, '60s and early '70s, and no escapes were reported as a result of that practice. During the early '50s, one trusted inmate took himself to the Gold Pan Bar for meals. The miscreant made no secret of the fact that he brought beer back to his cell as well. The sheriff left the door to the jail cell open during the day. He locked it at night only!

Building a second jail cell followed an arrest in 1952. The only cell until then was for men, but the suspects in the '52 case were two women picked up at Dillon's Wildwood Lodge and charged with car theft.* Since there was no cell at the Summit County Jail for women, they were transported to Leadville. Later that year, a cell for women was added.

Building the women's cell resulted in an unexpected benefit to county clerk Edna Dercum. A large closet in her office was located directly above the new cell. The installation of plumbing for the cell allowed the addition of a pipe going up to the clerk's closet. The availability of water meant that a duplicating machine could be installed in Edna's office. The need to type carbon copies decreased -- a reason to celebrate!

Outside, refurbished color murals enhanced the courthouse exterior. The scenes in the two pediments have been re-

---

* The Wildwood Lodge, originally erected in Old Dillon, was moved to Silverthorne when the Dillon Dam was under construction. It's now the Elks Lodge in Silverthorne.

painted twice. George Warren, aided by Harold Nelson, did a touch-up job in the late '40s or early '50s. Another touchup was done in 1959, in time for the Rush for the Rockies.

The later repainting was overseen by well-known artist and Breckenridge resident Jane Porter Robertson. Whether or not Robertson had a fear of heights is not known, but at the time of the repainting she was somewhat elderly, and over the years she may have learned not to trust wobbly ladders. She also may have been too modest or dignified to climb up a ladder, since a skirt – not trousers -- was a lady's usual attire.

Whatever the reason, Robertson oversaw the repainting, she didn't do it. With her feet planted solidly on terra firma, she stood on the ground and shouted instructions to Earl Knight Jr. as to which color should go where in the mosaics. Holes purposefully left in the mosaics indicated entrances to an adit (mining scene) and to a tunnel (railroad scene).

Differentiating between the two mosaics is difficult because they are so much alike. In the mining scene, the ground outside the adit entrance is lighter than the ground outside the tunnel entrance; perhaps this lighter color represents tailings. A darker gold "boulder" also rests on the "tailings." Speculation is that the boulder represents "Tom's Baby."

That's one big beautiful baby!
Miners Tom Groves and Harry J. Lytton found the now-famous "Tom's Baby" on July 27, 1887, at the Gold Flake Mine on Farncomb Hill east of Breckenridge. Weighing 13 lbs. 7 oz., the hefty nugget is Colorado's largest and one of the state's most beautiful specimens. It is on exhibit at the Denver Museum of Natural History.

So much to do, so little time

Earl Knight Jr., the courthouse mosaic painter, was a part-time housepainter/wallpaper hanger and the husband of county clerk Helen Knight. He was county sheriff for part of 1958 (he was appointed – not elected – due to the illness of then Sheriff Melvin Ray Loomis). For years, Knight was a member of the volunteer fire department. Knight's term as sheriff ranks as the shortest since Breckenridge gold discoverer Ruben J. Spaulding wore the territorial sheriff badge in 1859. (From 1859 until 1876 the title was territorial sheriff; after 1876 it was changed to county sheriff.)

Knight and county treasurer Frank Brown worked the Vulcan Mine on Baldy Mountain. Prior to becoming a part-time miner/prospector, Knight ran the Resurrection Mine in Leadville. He came by his love for mining naturally, for his father owned the Morning Star Mine on Baldy.

Knight demonstrated his artistic talent in another area besides mosaic painting – jewelry making. It was a natural choice since he had a supply of gold flakes from his mining operations at his disposal. Knight was typical of many Summit County residents who held various jobs, sometimes over the years and sometimes simultaneously.

Jailhouse Rock? No, Jailhouse Brick

Jail renovations seem endless. Perhaps it's because the jail's population doesn't peak or even plateau. It just grows, and as it grows so do its space requirements.

A major addition was constructed on the courthouse's west side in 1973. Referred to as the annex, the new section housed the main administrative office, behind which was the BOCC Hearing Room. Later, the countywide communications system was installed in the BOCC Room, so the commissioners met in the district courtroom when court was not in session. The peak in the annex's roof contains electrical and ventilation equipment.

Renovators shifted the jail from the basement to the top floor of the annex over the administrative offices. During some weekends in the 1980s when the jail was crowded with drunks, the inmates deliberately plugged up the toilets; when the county manager arrived at his office on Monday mornings, he was assaulted by stench, moisture and bits of raw sewage! By that time the custodian's apartment in the courthouse basement was just a memory. Had someone stayed in the building over night, perhaps less mischief would have ensued.

The jail was like a huge cage divided into cells within a very large room. The cells had windows to a hallway, referred to as the catwalk, and the catwalk had windows with screens to the outside. Inmates could be observed from the catwalk or from the end of the corridor that ran between the rows of cells. The jail was equipped with electric door locks that were operated by remote control. It also had a small exercise room outfitted with weight-lifting equipment.

The jail had three cells for trustees -- inmates on work release -- and smoke detectors were installed in their area. Whenever a minimum-security prisoner took a shower the detectors, which were fairly primitive and equally sensitive to steam and smoke, went off, triggering an alarm. Volunteers from the fire department would arrive ready to fight a blaze that never materialized. This situation existed for years. The sheriff's department believed that detectors, even faulty ones, were better than no detectors. Eventually, however, the fire department, frustrated by the false alarms, began charging for them. That expense supplied one of many incentives to build a new, state-of-the-art jail.

Although the jail was built to hold 15 people, busy weekends forced jailers to pack 50-60 people into the facility. This crowded condition, due largely to Judge Jewel Smith-Biddle's rigid stance on DUIs, kept the jail full on weekends. This sardine-can condition provided the primary impetus to build a new and much larger jail in 1987.

Wanted: Interior decorators

Insuring prisoner comfort is not a new challenge. The minutes of the May 20, 1882 BOCC meeting state that the commissioners, after duly inspecting the county jail, "pronounced it unsafe and instructed the county clerk to request the sheriff to remove the prisoners therein confined to Lake County for incarceration until jail could be thoroughly repaired. On motion, Commissioner [Chairman George] Ryan was empowered to see that county jail was *properly furnished* so as to make prisoners *comfortable*." (Italics added.)

The overcrowding grew so bad that inmates, with the help of the American Civil Liberties Union, filed a suit against the county. The county initially responded by moving some of its inmates to other county jails. That solution failed for two reasons: the increased expense and the time-consuming transport of prisoners.

Overcrowding presented only one problem; many others existed. The jail's fire-evacuation systems were outdated.

Neither the jail nor the courtrooms provided handicap accessibility. The final catalyst that got the wheels of progress turning was a federal court order demanding that a new jail be built -- fast!

The jail kitchen was built on the east end of the jail where the current entrance to the clerk and recorder's office is, but in the original courthouse. Adjacent to it on the north, just inside the present clerk and recorder's office, was the sheriff's personal office, and just north of that room was the undersheriff's office.

A solitary holding cell occupied the northwest corner of the jail. A prisoner had to be considered extremely dangerous, to others and to himself, to be confined to that cell. The prisoner was stripped, issued a bedroll (sheet and blanket) and, usually, denied food. The cell had no furniture, but it did have a toilet -- a hole that was flushed by a jailer on the outside who pushed a button.

In 1982, a chronic drunk from Silverthorne was arrested and put in the holding cell. With the one telephone call he was allowed to make, he called his wife to ask her to bond him out. She said no, so the inmate had to spend the night in solitary confinement. When the on-duty jailer went on his 10 p.m. rounds, he found the inmate hanging from a ceiling vent. The prisoner had torn the sheet into strips, then tied the strips into a rope with which he hanged himself.

The inmate's wife sued the county. She was awarded a nuisance settlement of $10,000. This incident was the impetus for the establishment of the county detox center.

Since this photograph was taken decades before smoking in public buildings was prohibited, most likely these men are not on a smoking break. Probably they are waiting for the doors to the Summit County Courthouse to open so they can go in and transact the day's business. Note the mural in the pediment.

One jail "renovation" was unexpected and unwanted. In the early '80s, an investigator failed to unload his 30/30 rifle before cleaning it. A round went off. It hit the door to the female cell block and left its mark.

What? Not More Changes!

Reconstruction wasn't restricted to the jail. Downstairs, the county commissioners set up shop in the northwest (paneled) section of the original basement. The apartment was taken out. The northeast corner contained the boiler room, a small room in which a freezer filled with TV dinners for the inmates was stored, and the buildings and grounds department head's very tiny office. The coal furnace was converted into a propane furnace and the coal chute was closed. Later the propane furnace was reconverted to use natural gas. The rest of the east side of the original basement housed the social services department (south), the two-story vault (middle) and the county nurses' office (north).

Prior to 1977, the Father Dyer United Methodist Church occupied the property due north of the courthouse. At that time, the ground behind the courthouse rose many feet higher than it does today and it sloped toward the church property. A bunker of sorts was built into the small hill. At first the bunker contained a coal bin. After the furnace conversion from coal to propane, the county used the concrete-lined coal bin as a storehouse for its records.

Over the years, the concrete deteriorated and water seeped slowly into the area. For some inexplicable reason, the person who oversaw the storage never said or did anything about the deteriorating condition. One year, in the middle of the '80s after a heavy snow winter and a wet spring, a worker opened the door to the bunker and stared in surprise at a soggy scene. A collapsed corner had allowed runoff water to drain in. Sodden unreadable papers stood in two feet of water. The documents, ruined beyond repair, had to be discarded. The day of the disappointing discovery, the "overseer" reportedly quit.

After the furnace conversion to gas, a shed was built on top of the bunker to house an emergency gas generator. This generator served only part of the courthouse, most importantly the communications department. The generator tested itself for 15 minutes every week, and it invariably performed like clockwork. Twice, though, when emergencies struck, the generator fired up perfectly but only worked for 20 minutes. No one had remembered to check its fuel supply! The generator has since been moved to a shed on the north side of the building that houses the buildings and grounds department. Its fuel supply is checked on a regular basis.

In 1978, the lower floor underwent several changes, because the BOCC Room and the county manager's office were "commandeered" by the communications department. Electronic doors were added to guarantee the security of that department. The county manager's office moved into the space previously occupied by the district court judge's office on the top floor. Information services/data processing relocated across the hall from the part of the communications office that occupied the lower floor of the annex.

Until the middle '70s, election equipment was stored in the county clerk and recorder's office. As the county grew, the office became congested. Moving the election equipment to the attic between the cupola and top floor seemed like a partial solution to the overcrowding problem. However, gaining access to the stored equipment became tricky. As late as the '80s, workers had to run a gauntlet created by employee lunches left to chill on the cool attic stairs. That section of the courthouse was so cold that it doubled as a refrigerator.

A small but important addition was made to the district courtroom on Jan. 2, 1980: a plaque that read Frances Harris Room was secured above the entry door. Frances, district court clerk for 21 years, worked under four judges. At the retirement party in her honor, the room was dedicated and the plaque affixed.

An 8-hour workday? What's that?

For several years, Frances did everything connected with the district court office except adjudicate: she filed cases, made up term dockets and collected support payments while simultaneously serving as jury commissioner and bailiff. Often her heavy workload required her to burn the midnight and weekend oil. It wasn't until the late '60s that she got help, starting with the assignment of other bailiffs at big jury trials. Marion Mueller and Helen Knight were two of the bailiffs to work with Frances.

Ever Changing - A Major Remodel in 1987

County officials initiated a major remodeling in 1987. In a project designed by Baker + Hogan Associates, the jail was relocated to the newly constructed Justice Center; its removal freed space for a greatly expanded clerk and recorder's office. The courtrooms moved to the Justice Center too. Moving those rooms and the jail meant that the county commissioners finally had their own hearing room. They now enjoy the use of the former district courtroom on the top floor. Changes to that room include the installation of a fire escape and a door to the fire escape as well as the installation of sprinklers. To protect the integrity of the original pressed-tin ceiling, planners had the sprinklers installed along the walls rather than the ceiling.

During this remodeling project, it became necessary to access the plumbing apparatus behind the men's bathroom in the basement. To the surprise of everyone, the area behind the bathroom (at the southwest corner where the annex joins the courthouse) was filled with old court records, newspapers and blueprints, papers that had been presumed lost or destroyed. How they got there is anyone's guess.

Courthouse staff played "musical rooms" upstairs. The rooms previously occupied by the jury/law library, bailiff/attorneys and judge's wardrobe became the county commissioners' private offices. Renovators installed an elevator shaft in the space previously occupied by the three-story vault stack. The money for the elevator came from a mineral-impact funds grant through the Colorado Department of Local Affairs. Portions of the vault stack not occupied by the elevator shaft hold storage vaults. The two-story vault was not touched. The back stairs also were redone in 1987.

Status Quo? Heck, No. More Facelifts!

After decades of use, plus exposure to the elements and ravages of salt for ice removal, the sandstone front steps leading to the courthouse's front door fell apart. Replacement of those steps in 1996, plus installation of three handrails (one going up the center and one along each side of the steps), created a new look for the entrance. The wooden shed that had housed tools and equipment for the groundskeeper was torn down. Staff reroofed the annex that year; they reroofed the original building the following year.

The latest facelift occurred in 1998, culminating in a grand reopening in December. Large-scale remodeling was done, especially in the basement. The much-needed expansion of many county offices had been made possible by the relocation of other offices to the new County Commons Center just south of Frisco. One office that moved was the communications department; it now has its own 15,000-sq.-ft. state-of-the-art communications center on the County Commons property. Its old space on the lower level of the original courthouse, now occupied by the employee lunchroom, still sports the old paneling.

A welcome and comfortable feeling greets visitors to the courthouse. At the same time, history wears a badge of importance in the building. The placement of Victorian furniture in the lobby captures a homey atmosphere. A quilt that depicts various Summit County places and industries is displayed prominently in the lobby. The significance of history also is featured in numerous old photos exhibited in various corridors and offices. Period carpeting and lots of plants complete the interior redecoration.

The Summit County Courthouse in 1910 stood ready to be occupied. Note the wooden shed that housed tools and equipment for the groundskeeper. The shed remained for 86 years. It was torn down in 1996 when the steps were replaced.

Section II: The People

Courthouse Characters

The popularity of winter sports has caused an economic boom in Summit County. Since the early '70s, people have flocked to this Rocky Mountain paradise to enjoy every kind of snow- and ice-related activity imaginable.

Many of these sports enthusiasts are young adults who come to play and work, but soon find that expenses are higher than anticipated and that to afford the pleasures of sport, they must work two or three jobs. Some lament this situation while others brag and obviously take pride in numbers: of jobs held, hours spent on the slopes or in the backcountry, hours (alarmingly few) slept.

To hear people talk, you'd think the phenomenon of multiple jobs were new. Not so. In the next sections you'll meet several characters who knew what it was like to have several employers. Sometimes economic conditions -- low pay versus high expenses -- required people to have multiple jobs. Sometimes the lack of population required it -- there were more essential jobs than workers to fill them. The county employees portrayed on the following pages were not exceptions to the multiple-job syndrome, they were practitioners of it.

Summit Countians didn't just work hard. Most played hard and many drank hard. They wanted to be rewarded for doing a long and hard day's work.

Following are snippets from some of their stories.

Good timing! Just one month after fire destroyed three county buildings, among them the old county courthouse, a celebration took place. A flag-raising ceremony on the courthouse lawn in August 1936 brought cheer and uplifted spirits. The celebration marked the formal annexation into the State of Colorado of a disputed strip of land, including Breckenridge, known as No Man's Land. After the fire's devastation, citizens welcomed a positive experience to assuage the gloom that hung over the town.

Stories: County Officials, Staff and Events

For about a month in 1957, the county courthouse served as the cultural and entertainment center for Breckenridge residents. In that year, a television translator with a temporary gas generator was installed on Baldy Mountain. Dedicated and hearty volunteers made daily treks up Baldy to fill the generator with gas and fire it up so the translator would work.

Breckenridge residents gathered at the courthouse to watch the one television set there. They watched the news at 6 p.m. and remained glued to the set until the generator ran out of gas at about 10 p.m. The next night the TV viewers returned to watch until, once again, the generator ran out of fuel.

This gas generator provided the power to run TVs prior to the erection of the first booster station in the Upper Blue Valley -- the one on Baldy. Members of the volunteer fire department installed the auxiliary station. They cut trees for the electricity-generated booster station and cleared the path for the power line running to the station.

꙳꙳꙳ ꙳꙳꙳ ꙳꙳꙳ ꙳꙳꙳ ꙳꙳꙳ ꙳꙳꙳ ꙳꙳꙳

In the late 1960s or early '70s, a woman filed charges against Dr. Thor Jorgenson, an osteopath who practiced in his Frisco home, for inducing an abortion. People had long suspected the doctor performed that then-illegal procedure. Until the woman pressed charges, however, no proof existed on which to try him. In this case, Jorgenson readied the woman for an abortion to be completed in Denver, then put her on a

bus bound for that city. While on the bus, the woman hemor-
rhaged and nearly died.

The State Health Department, in its investigation of the
case, found a fetus preserved in formaldehyde in a bottle in the
doctor's garage. Officials seized the bottle as evidence and
used it against the defendant at his trial. Based on such indis-
putable evidence, the jury found Jorgenson guilty and recom-
mended that he serve time in the Canon City prison. The
dumbfounded jury learned later that the doctor never spent a
minute in jail and never lost his license. He merely moved his
practice from Frisco to Georgetown and then later to another
Colorado town.

In the possible event the case would be appealed, over-
turned or otherwise reopened, the bottle with the fetus was
kept in the three-story district court vault until 1973. At that
time it was turned over to the coroner, Olin Mueller, who put
it in the two-story vault for continued safe keeping.

While the fetus resided in a county vault, other dead
bodies were kept in Mueller's yellow station wagon (one of the
two ambulances in the county) as well as in the barn at Whatley Ranch where Mueller was caretaker. Since Summit County
had no mortuary, the coroner either had to transport a corpse
to Idaho Springs, Leadville or Hot Sulphur Springs or wait until
someone from one of those mortuaries drove to Summit
County to pick it up. On rare occasions, Mueller transported
corpses as far away as Fort Collins and Grand Junction.

Depending on the weather, a ride to Idaho Springs
could be a harrowing experience. Since the Eisenhower Tunnel wasn't completed and opened until 1973, drivers had to
travel over Loveland Pass to get to Idaho Springs. At times the

road conditions grew so bad that Mueller waited before attempting a treacherous drive. Fortunately, because of the county's cold and dry winter climate, the coroner's unique "storage units" didn't pose a preservation problem.

Stored corpses were one thing, but pictures of them were another. Reportedly, Mueller took and kept pictures of the dead bodies -- some clothed, some naked -- and passed the gruesome photos around at Christmas parties. This disgusted many of the guests but delighted the coroner.

In addition to his coroner duties, Mueller drove a school bus (as did his wife, Marion). He was popular with his charges because of the weekly rewards of Butterfingers he gave on Friday to every student who hadn't missed a day of school during the week. Prior to his driving job, Mueller was a cook at the high school (so was Marion). He served on the county school board -- old-timers agree that conflict of interest didn't matter in those days -- and he was bailiff at the county court (while Marion was bailiff at the district court).

The Muellers obviously found their contact with children rewarding and pleasant, because for years they sponsored annual fishing contests for grade-schoolers at the Whatley Ranch pond. Youngsters eagerly anticipated these springtime contests in which everyone was a winner.

Olin was a charter member of the Veterans of Foreign Wars Post and of the Summit County Veterans Memorial Post - American Legion. On July 30, 1977, shortly after the founding of the Posts, a sudden and horrendous windstorm hit the county with a vengeance. Several sailboats on Lake Dillon capsized, all empty except one. Ten unsuspecting friends -- eight on deck and two in the cabin -- socialized on board that vessel. Then the wind hit, flipping the boat. Wind and waves tossed those on deck overboard.

One woman tried to escape from the cabin. She got tangled in the lines of the sails, so she returned to the "safety" of an air pocket in the compartment. Some of the men tried to right the boat but, in so doing, burst the air bubble. The craft sank. Only 1,600 feet of water separated the party-goers from the Dillon Marina. People on shore witnessed the accident and hurried out in boats to rescue those in the water.

Officers from the sheriff's department arrived first to search for the boat and victims. Members of Summit County Search and Rescue were called in the next day to help in the mission. They used drag lines with grappling hooks on the ends to find the vessel, to no avail. Next came the use of precise, high-powered survey instruments called theodolites in combination with sightings, again with no success. Tests on drift currents and the use of sonar followed.

By Aug. 3, Search and Rescue took over the operation. An underwater TV camera was lowered into the lake on Aug. 10. The boat was spotted on Aug. 11. Workers brought up one victim immediately. They moved the vessel to shallower water on Aug. 12, and on Aug. 13 extricated the second victim from the cabin. The rescue mission took 15 days and 2,640 man-hours from start to finish. It involved local and Front Range deep-water divers.

The operation took so long -- primarily because sightings by onlookers were off by 300 feet -- that members of the two Posts constantly asked Olin if the bodies had been freed yet. Invariably he answered, "Nope, they're still on the bottom playing with a full deck."

At the time of the accident, no Summit County Dive Rescue Team existed, only Search and Rescue. The latter enjoyed support from county government to the extent that it had its own line item in the county budget. The money went primarily for insurance and equipment.

After the accident, State Patrolman Dave Batura started the wheels turning for the formation of a Dive Rescue Team. The county revamped its budget, and partial financing of that group as well as of Search and Rescue became part of the sheriff's department budget.

Although the two groups receive the lion's share of their funding from grants and donations, county money still covers their telephone, heat, radio-battery, workman's compensation and vehicle-fuel expenses. Both headquarter in the county barn.

᠁ ᠁ ᠁ ᠁ ᠁ ᠁ ᠁

Voters elected Marty Florhs coroner after Mueller. She cleaned out the vault and properly disposed of the bottled fetus, as well as one or two boxes of cremated remains. Curiously, a black metal box with a tooth in it continued to "reside" in the vault long after the other items were cleared away.

Competent and professional, Flohrs wasn't as colorful a character as her predecessor, but she outshone him when it came to holding practice triage sessions. A masterful make-up artist, she used all the theatrical tricks of the trade -- putty, wax, fake blood, etc. -- on her volunteer victims to achieve a high degree of realism. Not only were the victims made up to look like they'd suffered deep cuts or painful bruises, but they were prompted on how to act as though they'd had heart attacks, seizures or other health problems. Under her tenure, triage simulation for mass casualties was eerily real, educational and unforgettable.

~~ ~~ ~~ ~~ ~~ ~~ ~~

Before the mid-1970s, workers in the county clerk's office rubbed elbows with those employed in the motor vehicle department. Often their functions overlapped and at especially busy times, most notably license-renewal time, they'd fill in for one another.

One extremely busy year in the early 1970s, the motor vehicle department generated so much activity that the office ran out of license plates. Back then, the department mailed license-renewal notices to all vehicle owners in mid-December. Owners had until the end of February to get their new license plates (not stickers as today), plates that bore the prefix ZL. When Summit County ran out of license plates, the Colorado secretary of state authorized Park County to share its plates with its northern neighbor. A problem ensued: Park County plates began with ZD, a prefix reportedly unacceptable to some Summit County residents.

Staffers learned their lessons. They issued more ZL plates and people renewed their licenses earlier. Eventually, license-renewal dates were changed to fall on the anniversary of original issuance, thus spreading the work over the year. County old-timers still cherish their ZL plates. Most plates issued now start either with three letters beginning with a W or with a Z1L or ZR prefix.

A statewide motor-vehicle registration system was devised in 1909. It reserved license-plate numbers 49,901 to 50,000 for Summit County vehicles. That was sufficient for a while. By Aug. 1, 1917, 56 cars were registered. But by 1924,

176 cars, four trucks and four motorcycles were registered. The numbering system, changed by 1926 to accommodate all those drivers bitten by the auto bug, provided an allotment of 500 for Summit County.

That new allotment didn't prove to be sufficient for long. The county issued 314 licenses in 1929. Most of the licenses were for Fords, followed closely by Chevrolets -- this despite the nonexistence of Ford or Chevy dealers in the county. Having a Dodge dealership in the county probably accounts for the 50 Dodges licensed in 1929.

Ignoring the fact that automobile ownership increased rapidly and quickly lost its novelty, *The Summit County Journal* continued to report each new acquisition.

※ ※ ※ ※ ※ ※ ※

Solid brass spittoons, strategically placed by the janitor, were in abundance in the courthouse for decades, used by visitors and staff alike. In 1949, while county clerk Edna Dercum helped a man fill out his license application, she heard a strange but not unfamiliar sound. The young father's 4-year-old son had availed himself of a spittoon -- for a potty!

As Edna wrote in her book *It's easy, Edna, it's downhill all the way*, "when you gotta go, you gotta go."

※ ※ ※ ※ ※ ※ ※

One interviewee remembered that a sharpshooter served as deputy county sheriff and, later in the 1940s, as county assessor. Ed Stuart, primarily when he was deputy sheriff, traveled around the country appearing at shows to promote

Remington arms. In one of his acts he tossed silver dollars in the air and shot holes through them before they hit the ground.

༺༺༺༺༺༺༺

One day, county motor-vehicle examiner Russell Mumford accompanied a man to the county clerk's office. As was his custom, Mumford informed clerk Edna Dercum that the man had passed the driving test and thus should be issued a temporary license. A permanent license would be issued by the state at a later date.

Unlike his custom, however, Mumford stayed in Edna's office instead of returning to his own desk in the basement. After the applicant received his license and left, Mumford said to Edna, "Boy, he sure am stupid."

"Stupid?" responded Edna. "Why do you say that? He passed the test, didn't he?"

"Yeah, but he didn't know what a presbyterian is," Mumford replied.

"What does a Presbyterian have to do with a driver's exam?" asked a perplexed Edna.

"A presbyterian is them people what walks across the street," a smug Mumford answered.

༺༺༺༺༺༺༺

County clerk and recorder Zelda Ashlock was a courthouse fixture from 1961 to 1975. Known for her steel-willed personality, Zelda ruled the clerk's office with an iron fist. A sign on the cork bulletin board in her office read "I don't give a

Edna Dercum began her political career in 1949 when she shared a ticket with her father-in-law, "Opa" Dercum. Opa, a Republican, ran for county clerk; Edna, a mugwump, ran as his "temporary" deputy. The Dercums won handily. Edna had agreed to serve only until Opa could find a permanent deputy, a few months at the most. But two weeks into his term, Opa died. One week after Opa's funeral, the county commissioners appointed Edna county clerk. So popular was Edna that when she ran for the position in the next election, she won, five to one. Edna retired from politics on May 1, 1952. Her next career was as a ski instructor and inter- nationally-known racer. Photo courtesy of Edna Dercum.

damn how they do it in Denver, this is Summit County." The sign was meant for Denver residents who'd try to register their cars at the Summit County Motor Vehicle Department.

While her courthouse demeanor was stern and inflexible, outside the work environment Zelda enjoyed high regard as a nice and good person "who, if she found a need, filled it."

Apparently, Zelda's strictness applied not only to her dealings with people, but with the clock as well. One day, promptly at noon, she slammed the door to the vault closed, locking Ray McGinnis inside. McGinnis, a surveyor, spent a lot of time in the vault and clerk's office. He knew Zelda's deserved reputation for punctuality, so he wasn't worried about getting out.

Sure enough, the first thing Zelda did upon her return after lunch exactly one hour later was open the vault. McGinnis was ready. It would be an understatement to say that the sight of McGinnis, who stood with his nose pressed against the vault door, startled Zelda. She let out a scream, stepped back and toppled over a desk.

"What are you doing in there?" she demanded. Replied McGinnis, "You locked the door without checking to see if the vault was empty." Zelda's red face attested to the fact that she was guilty as accused.

Zelda was a chain-smoker; a cloud of smoke hung permanently over her desk. While the smell of smoke didn't bother her, reportedly the odor of hippies did. Whenever they entered the clerk's office, Zelda got out a can of Lysol spray, aimed it in their direction and pushed on the nozzle. She sprayed anything and everything they touched, including pencils.

It was fortunate that smoke didn't bother Zelda, for she frequently tended bar at the Lucky Horseshoe in Dillon, a saloon owned by her boyfriend. While it might seem strange for a county clerk to moonlight as a bartender, it didn't seem unusual to Zelda. Before her husband, Henry, county roads supervisor, died in 1951, she and he owned and operated a mercantile and liquor store and a gas station in Dillon.

Although Zelda physically left the courthouse in 1975, her name and spirit stayed on: the first computer to make a home in the building was nicknamed Zelda.

The difference between the old and new so captivated famous photographer Otto Westerman that he just had to snap this shot. To the left an old log cabin with a rock chimney stands in contrast to the $43,000 courthouse in its stately splendor. Far right is the Engle Brothers Exchange Bank in which the county offices had once been located.

Stories: Court, a Judge and a Victim

In the 1860s, Summit County held a court session once a year on the fourth Tuesday of July. Later, the court remained in session all that week. The session -- called Court Week -- marked the occasion for a dance. Fiddles and an organ supplied the music for the dance.

〰〰〰〰〰〰〰

A county employee found a pack belonging to miner Leonard M. Thomas of Breckenridge in a corner during the courthouse's 1987 renovation. A murder victim, Thomas was a Union soldier, a private in the Civil War -- gunshot ankle wound and all -- and a former resident of Pennsylvania. In his satchel were nine photographs, fish line, a pouch of champagne-flavored plug tobacco, an Excelsior diary (with notes from Feb. 28, 1891 to Oct. 8, 1892), a fountain pen, a Memoranda [notebook], a pension certificate (he received $6 a month as of Nov. 3, 1884, for that ankle injury), a letter from Maud Hale dated Oct. 14, 1892, and a Workman's Monthly Time Book listing Thomas's workdays, primarily at the Gold Dust Lode, from June through December 1885.

Thomas wrote in his diary that he was part owner of the Ouray location in 1886. Elsewhere he listed his name with seven others: Irwin/Irving/Ervin Howbert (locator of the Howbert Lode on May 12, 1892), H.A. Watson (Four Boy Lode, May 23, 1892; Alymick Lode, June 12, 1892), J.A. Watson, Lewis Wilson (St. Kilda Lode, May 12, 1892), L.P. Snavely (Sailor Boy Lode, May 12, 1892), Al Grisham (Turk Lode, May 23, 1892) and William Berry (Iron Lode, May 12, 1892). Thomas listed himself as discoverer of the Orient Lode on May 23,

1892. C. Willsworth and K.D. Smith were mentioned as discoverers of the Atlantic Lode on Feb. 12, 1892.

A few pages later Thomas wrote "Santa Rita, L.M. Thomas." He referred to the Santa Rita again when he wrote, "To all whom it may concern and in particular (followed by a blank line). We hereby warn any person from either setting any stakes or digging any holes on the surface ground of the Santa Rita claim. Or in any way trespassing on said property." Obviously, Thomas's claim was being contested or threatened. But by whom? By one or more of the men on the list?

Theories about Thomas's murder abound. Could one or more persons (perhaps mentioned in his diary) have jumped his claim and killed him? Was Thomas aware of a cattle-rustling scheme? Did he plan to snitch all he knew to the county court judge? Was Thomas caught fooling around with another miner's wife? If so, did the victimized husband shoot Thomas in a fit of jealousy and rage?

No suspect was implicated in the murder, which occurred sometime after the middle of October 1892, so no trial took place. However, Thomas's pack was kept as evidence should ever the need arise.*

〜〜〜〜〜〜〜
〜〜〜〜〜〜〜

One of the better known county court judges was Lynn Carter. For a while Carter worked at the Climax Mine during the day and attended college at night. That became too much to handle, so he quit his job to enroll in school full time, even-

---

* Thomas's satchel, donated to the Summit Historical Society, is exhibited in the Edwin Carter Museum, 111 North Ridge Street in Breckenridge. Other items once housed in the courthouse and now displayed in the museum include the heavy iron door to the county's first jail and animal heads that had lined the walls in the commissioners' room.

tually earning a bachelor of science degree. Upon graduation, Carter went to work for the FBI. After retirement from the FBI, he became county court judge and, at various times, dispatcher in the sheriff's office, part-time jailer and sewer-plant operator for three or four of the county's facilities. Following his retirement from the bench in the late '70s, Carter attended the University of Denver Law School. He later opened a legal practice in Denver.

Locals know Judge Carter best for what many say he held sacred -- his daily afternoon naps and nips. Since he frequently partied until the wee hours of the morning, he reportedly needed afternoon snoozes to compensate for his lack of nighttime shuteye. This hard-drinking portrait of Carter was painted by most people who knew him (and, in some instances, socialized with him). However, one co-worker, who saw him daily, stated that she never saw him drink or sleep on the job.

Despite his FBI training, Carter was caught off-guard once. One night as Carter sat at a local bar, a patron recognized him as the judge who had slapped him with a hefty sentence. The sight of the judge so enraged the patron that he walked over to him and punched him, knocking Carter off his bar stool!

Like Jewel Smith-Biddle, Carter earned a reputation as a hanging judge. He demanded respect for himself and the court system from everyone at all times. He refused to tolerate unpreparedness; those who appeared before him quickly learned to have their acts together. Parties found guilty, especially of DUI or shoplifting, received severe treatment, often time in jail. Carter had a penchant for handing down tough sentences.

Carter received credit as the first county judge to give jail time for DUIs. He also spearheaded the county's first community-service program, well before the state instituted one. The concept behind community service was that those convicted of lesser crimes could serve either all or part of their sentences helping the community. This reduced expenses because fewer people spent time in jail. Usually, a nonprofit or government agency benefited the most from this service.

One day two men cited by a wildlife official for fishing in the Blue River without licenses appeared in court before Judge Carter. Both claimed they had licenses but just didn't carry them when fishing.

Carter asked the first man if he had his license prior to being cited. "Yes, sir," the man replied. He asked the same question of the second man. "No, sir," was his reply, "I got it after."

Carter found both men guilty of the same crime, but gave them different community-service sentences: Man #1, because he lied, got the maximum; Man #2, rewarded for his honesty, got the minimum. Both did their service at the Snake River Water Treatment Plant painting, mowing and doing odd jobs.

In Carter's day, it was hard to summon up enough people to field a jury. It was so bad that once the judge appointed a surprised nursing mother to a jury. As the mother sat in the jury box, her 10-month-old son sat on the judge's lap, happily chewing on the gavel between nursing breaks. Everyone enjoyed Carter's humor when, after the baby let out a particularly loud burp, the judge declared, "Juror #7 didn't like that remark!"

Stories: Jail Inmates

Probably the most notorious inmate held at the Summit County Jail was Johnny McDaniels. Born at the Big-4 Mine at Green Mountain, McDaniels started his career in crime at a young age. He was accused of killing his brother-in-law and blowing up the Heeney post office and of planning to kill his niece with a bomb. While McDaniels didn't succeed in driving the Heeney postmaster crazy (he shot at him and missed, whether or not purposefully isn't known), he did manage to drive the man out of the county.

McDaniels committed many crimes, was jailed many times and escaped from jail nearly as many times. He was captured and jailed in Summit County on a fugitive warrant from Eagle County. At the time of McDaniels's apprehension in 1951, the ceiling of the Summit County Jail was lathe and plaster. So were the interior walls. Fortunately the exterior walls were brick.

McDaniels tried to escape -- unsuccessfully. His first try was via the floor, the second via a wall. The second try terminated at the exterior brick wall. That didn't mean the end to subsequent attempts, however.

During one escape attempt, McDaniels disassembled some plumbing. When he returned to his cell, he held a large heavy pipe. In his hands the pipe became a fearsome weapon. McDaniels refused to surrender the pipe until he spoke to county attorney Robert Theobald. Sheriff Ray Loomis brought Theobald to the jail, and a short while later Theobald succeeded in calming down an agitated McDaniels. After that bungled escape try, a steel plate was installed above the ceiling.

McDaniels and Trouble (with a capital T) gravitated toward each other. One evening he unscrewed the light bulb from the socket in his cell and replaced it with pennies, causing all the lights in the courthouse to go out. County clerk Edna Dercum had stayed late to proofread the deeds she had typed earlier in the day. The episode so spooked Edna that she uncharacteristically left the office without finishing her work.

In due time, McDaniels was transferred back to Eagle County. When the authorities came to escort him, an Eagle County officer told Sheriff Loomis there was no way McDaniels could escape from Eagle's new, state-of-the-art jail. Loomis was doubtful, and rightfully so, for a long, beveled steel chisel was found under McDaniels's mattress after he left. The day after the transfer, all of Eagle County's jailbirds flew the coop except McDaniels. Asked what happened to the other prisoners, McDaniels innocently replied, "What other guys?"

McDaniels eventually landed in Central City where he got mixed up with an unscrupulous mine promoter. His troubles ended permanently when he became the victim rather than the perpetrator. He and a mine co-worker were shot as they sat in a pickup truck. The vehicle and their bodies were unceremoniously pushed down a mine shaft. A Volkswagen was dumped on top of them for good measure!

〰〰〰〰〰〰〰

In 1976, the inmates in Cell 2 -- a burglar and a two-time rapist -- used the handles of their toothbrushes to scrape out the mortar around two cinder blocks. They had planned to remove the blocks to gain access to the catwalk, then to break out an exterior window off the catwalk and escape. The plan almost worked.

Fortunately for the safety of area residents, the felons made a noisy mistake. Instead of quietly pulling the cinder blocks forward and gently placing them on the floor of their cell, the men pushed them out. The blocks fell with loud clunks onto the floor of the catwalk. Fortunately, again, the jail was wired for sound. The night watchman heard the 3 a.m. crashes and acted fast enough to abort the inmates' escape.

〰〰〰〰〰〰〰

A mole surfaced in early 1983. It seems that two trustees (work-release inmates) collaborated on an escape plan with two inmates – David Gross, in on a burglary charge, and Mark Decault, jailed for assault. One of the trustees was responsible for bringing the inmates' TV dinners up from the freezer in the basement to be heated in the jail's kitchen on the main floor. The freezer was located just outside the door to the buildings and grounds department's office. It was easy for the trustee to slip into the office, grab a hacksaw blade, conceal it in his uniform and take it to Gross and Decault.

Over a two-week period, the cellmates used the blade to saw the expanded metal in front of their cell window. They hid the blade along the side of the window when a jailer was around, covering it with toothpaste the same color as the paint on their cell's wall. They also used toothpaste to fill in the holes made by the blade.

When the evening of the planned escape arrived, the trustee who stole the blade unlocked a screen on the inside of one of the catwalk's exterior windows. The other trustee, however, doublecrossed the two inmates and alerted the jailer. After the cellmates popped out the expanded-metal screen, got out of their cell, opened the screen on the catwalk window and jumped out, they found themselves face to face with officers from the Summit County Sheriff's Department and the Breckenridge Police Department. One practically landed in the arms of a waiting officer, while the other ran a short distance before being overtaken by lawmen.

≈ ≈ ≈ ≈ ≈ ≈ ≈

Early in 1984, police stopped a 25-year-old woman in Frisco at 10 a.m. on a warrant arrest. As was the custom then for those picked up on warrants for lesser crimes, the arresting officer permitted the woman to drive herself to the jail. At the jail, the woman was allowed to make one telephone call. She called her boyfriend at Copper Mountain and asked him to post her bail. He refused, so she was to be booked and jailed.

Before the required papers were filled out, however, the woman took advantage of a lapse in the booking officer's attention. She bolted out the front door, got into her car and drove away at a high rate of speed. Her timing was excellent, for most of the officers were in the parking lot at the back of the courthouse washing their cars. By the time the woman reached Tenmile Canyon on the way to Copper Mountain, she had 10 patrolmen pursuing her!

The woman exited Interstate 70 at Copper and pulled into a parking lot, whereupon she was immediately surrounded and blocked in by her pursuers. Highway patrol sergeant Darrell Clark ordered her to get out of her vehicle. She refused to comply. Clark broke the driver's side window, reached in, opened the door and yanked the woman out of her car. She was then taken back to the courthouse in a patrol car.

Not only did she not elude capture, but additional and more serious charges, such as escape, were put on her arrest record.

〜〜〜〜〜〜〜
〜〜〜〜〜〜〜

There was one successful, but short-lived, escape from the annex jail. In late 1983 or early 1984, a hardened criminal assaulted deputy jailer Bruce Ferrar, knocking him unconscious and nearly killing him. During his exercise period, the inmate had removed the weights from the ends of a barbell. He returned to his cell with the bar hidden in his clothes. Later, when Ferrar opened the inmate's cell door to escort him somewhere, the criminal bashed the deputy over the head and took his keys.

Craig Stanley, a work-release trustee, saw the commotion and rushed to the jailer's aid, probably saving his life. Nevertheless, the inmate managed to escape through the back door.

A major manhunt ensued. Two days later, a Breckenridge Police officer found the escapee holed up in a vacant house. From that time on, weight-lifting equipment was banned from the jail.

The winter of 1911/12 stretched on into summer. Proudly posing outside the Summit County Courthouse on June 17, 1912, are four of Breckenridge's finest. From the left are Dr. C.E. Condon, merchants Watson and Watson, and jeweler George C. Smith.

Conclusion

The story of Summit County's historic 1910 courthouse is not just a bricks-and-mortar recitation of additions, moves and renovations. It is also a story of people -- public-spirited citizens who clamored for the building; commissioners, architects and laborers who designed and built the structure; county personalities who worked or lived in the facility; researchers who used information stored in the building. People make the stately building come alive and take on a personality of its own.

The building commands notice for its beauty. That it is a loved and well-cared-for structure is obvious even to the casual observer. This care and attention lend a welcome and warm feel to the building.

Yet the building is also a place where judges handed down unpopular decisions and where tempers raged. And it's a building that harbors secrets -- some that the author chose not to reveal. Forced amorous attentions behind closed doors and illicit sex in the judge's quarters are just some of the secrets the building still keeps.

While people left their stamp on the building, the building had an impact on the people. Just as the heavy handedness of a jailer contrasted with the inviting smile of a clerk, the warmth of the oak-trimmed interior contrasted with the coldness of the jail cells' metal doors. By living or working in the courthouse, Summit County residents had their lives enriched. Conversely, the building resonates with the personalities of those same residents.

The Summit Historical Society's Year 2000 Christmas ornament features this drawing of the Summit County Courthouse. Printed above the drawing is "1910 - 2000, 90th Anniversary"; below the drawing is "Summit County Courthouse, Breckenridge, Colorado." The glossy metallic gold ball with black print is the Society's tenth ornament. This sketch and three others preceding it were drawn by Dave Koop of Silverthorne, Colorado.

Index

Sources

Aldrich, John K., *Ghosts of Summit County,* 1986, Centennial Graphics, Lakewood, CO 80214, 45-46.

Brown, Robert L., *Colorado Ghost Towns,* July 1972, The Caxton Printers, Ltd., Caldwell, ID 83605, 54, 56-57.

Carey, Julia, "Greed buries former county seat," *Timberland,* Feb. 1985, 11.

Carter, Edwin, museum of, 111 North Ridge Street, Breckenridge, CO 80424.

Clawson, Janet Marie, Nomination form to the National Register of Historic Places Inventory, U.S. Department of the Interior, Heritage Conservation and Recreation Service, Oct. 29, 1980.

Colorado History Now, newsletter of the Colorado Historical Society, January 2000, 10.

Daily Journal, Oct. 5, 1881; Sept. 26, 1886.

Daugherty, John, *Cultural Resource Inventories for Summit County, Colorado 1974 and 1975; Part II, Survey of Historic Mines and Mining Camps - Swan River, French Creek,* 1980, Summit Historical Society, Dillon, CO 80435.

Dempsey, Stanley and Fell, James E., *Mining the Summit,* 1986, University of Oklahoma Press, Norman, OK, 24.

Dercum, Edna Strand, *It's easy, Edna, it's downhill all the way,* 1981, Sirpos Press, Dillon, CO 80435, 103-105, 106-107.

Dyer, John Lewis, *Snow-Shoe Itinerant,* reprinted in 1975 by the Father Dyer United Methodist Church, Breckenridge, CO 80424, 143-144.

Father Dyer United Methodist Church brochure, Breckenridge, CO 80424.

Fiester, Mark, *Blasted Beloved Breckenridge,* 1973, Pruett Publishing Company, Boulder, CO 80302, 52, 58-59, 61, 106-108, 129-131, 163-164, 169.

Fleming, Naomi, letter to the Board of [Summit] County [CO] Commissioners, Aug. 5, 1985.

"Genuine Colorado," 1996/97 Breckenridge Vacation Planner, Breckenridge Resort Chamber, Breckenridge, CO 80424, 18.

Gilliland, Mary Ellen, *Breckenridge!* 1988, Alpenrose Press, Silverthorne, CO 80498, 4, 25, 46, 52. *Frisco! A Colorful Colorado Community,* 1984, Alpenrose Press, Silverthorne, CO 80498, 11-12. *Summit, A Gold Rush History of Summit County, Colorado,* 1980, Alpenrose Press, Silverthorne, CO 80498, 40-43, 57, 59, 231-232, 266.

Hall, Frank, *History of the State of Colorado,* Volume IV, 1895, The Blakely Printing Company, Chicago, 325 ,331.

Hovelsen, Leif, *The Flying Norseman,* 1983, National Ski Hall of Fame Press, Ishpeming, MI, 36.

LaBaw, Wallace L., *NAH-OON-KARA, The Gold of Breckenridge,* 1965, Big Mountain Press, Denver.

Maps of Breckenridge: 1886, 1890, 1892, 1896, 1900, 1902

Miller, Lyle, "Earliest Automobiling in Colorado: 1899-1904," *Colorado Heritage,* Autumn 1999, Colorado Historical Society, Colorado History Museum, Denver, CO 80203, 34.

Miller, T. Alex, "Breckenridge Architecture: Building Blocks of History, *Breckenridge Magazine,* Summer 1994, Breckenridge, CO 80424, 23.

Montezuma Millrun, Oct. 7, 1882.

Nicholls, Maureen and Tisdall, Nancy, "Centennial Historic Building Tour and Ice Cream Social" guide, Breckenridge Centennial Commission, Breckenridge, CO 80424, figure 2.

Noel, Thomas J., *Buildings of Colorado,* 1997, Oxford University Press, New York, 458, 461.

Pritchard, Sandra F., Ph.D., *Roadside Summit, Part II: The Human Landscape,* 1992, Summit Historical Society, Dillon, CO 80435, 69-70, 130.

Rocky Mountain News [The], May 2, 1880.

Signal [The], Summit Public Radio membership newsletter, Spring 1999, 1.

Summit County Commissioners Record, <u>1862-1878</u>, 24, 32-35, 37-39, 41, 46-51, 52, 59, 61, 67-68, 70, 85, 130, 136, 148, 163, 173, 175-176, 178, 182-183, 210-211, 217, 223, 235, 241, 253, 262, 280, 308, 310, 332, 339, 364, 370. <u>Book 3: Jan. 1, 1882 - Sept. 3, 1900</u>, 9, 19, 27, 70, 97, 127, 137, 160, 171, 178-179, 183, 191-192, 231, 234, 249, 285, 289, 389, 416, 418, 476, 531, 535-537, 539-540, 546, 549, 552, 557, 566. <u>Book 4: Sept. 4, 1900 - Jan. 10, 1912</u>, 11, 15, 25, 62, 78, 82, 94, 96, 105, 121-122, 131, 143, 155-156, 177, 184, 192, 198, 201, 213, 220, 228, 239-240, 360-363, 384-390, 392-393, 397-401, 411-412, 418, 421-422, 430-431.

Summit County Courthouse cornerstone.

Summit County History class, author's notes; Rebecca Waugh, teacher.

Summit County Journal, Jan. 14, 1888, Oct. 7, 1899, Nov. 4, 1899, Dec. 9, 1900, Jan. 4, 1908; July 24, 1909; July 31, 1909; Aug. 7, 1909; March 5, 1910; March 12, 1910; March 19, 1910; Feb. 28, 1930; July 10, 1936; Aug. 7, 1936; Aug. 6, 1948; Dec. 24, 1954.

Summit County Leader, March 3, 1888.

Summit County Lode Records, Book H, 438.

Summit County Official Bonds and Commissions and Pre-Exemption Records, Book D.

Summit County Pre-Exemption Records, Book E. Book F. Book L, 332.

Summit County Pre-Exemption Water Claims, Book K, 98.

Summit Historical Society artifact archives, photo archives, printed-material archives.

Theobald, Lois, *Thar's GOLD in them thar hills!,* 6, 29.

Thomas, Leonard M., diary of (Feb. 28, 1891 - Oct. 8, 1892).

Waugh, Rebecca, Historical Walking Tour Guides of North and South Main Streets in Breckenridge, 1997, Town of Breckenridge, CO 80424.

Women as tall as our mountains, 1976, 28.